Impact Evaluation in Firms and Organizations

Impact Evaluation in Firms and Organizations

With Applications in R and Python

Martin Huber

The MIT Press
Cambridge, Massachusetts
London, England

The MIT Press
Massachusetts Institute of Technology
77 Massachusetts Avenue, Cambridge, MA 02139
mitpress.mit.edu

© 2025 Massachusetts Institute of Technology

All rights reserved. No part of this book may be used to train artificial intelligence systems or reproduced in any form by any electronic or mechanical means (including photocopying, recording, or information storage and retrieval) without permission in writing from the publisher.

The MIT Press would like to thank the anonymous peer reviewers who provided comments on drafts of this book. The generous work of academic experts is essential for establishing the authority and quality of our publications. We acknowledge with gratitude the contributions of these otherwise uncredited readers.

This book was set in Times New Roman by Westchester Publishing Services. Printed and bound in the United States of America.

Library of Congress Cataloging-in-Publication Data

Names: Huber, Martin, 1980- author
Title: Impact evaluation in firms and organizations : with applications in R and Python / Martin Huber.
Description: Cambridge, Massachusetts : The MIT Press, [2025] | Includes bibliographical references and index.
Identifiers: LCCN 2024038920 (print) | LCCN 2024038921 (ebook) | ISBN 9780262552929 paperback | ISBN 9780262383905 epub | ISBN 9780262383912 pdf
Subjects: LCSH: Decision making–Data processing | Quantitative research | R (Computer program language) | Python (Computer program language)
Classification: LCC HD30.23 .H79 2025 (print) | LCC HD30.23 (ebook) | DDC 658.4/030285–dc23/eng/20250115
LC record available at https://lccn.loc.gov/2024038920
LC ebook record available at https://lccn.loc.gov/2024038921

10 9 8 7 6 5 4 3 2 1

EU product safety and compliance information contact is: mitp-eu-gpsr@mit.edu

To my family and friends.

Contents

		Preface and Acknowledgments	ix
1		**Introduction**	1
2		**Basics of Impact Evaluation**	7
	2.1	The Fundamental Problem of Impact Evaluation	7
	2.2	Characterizing the Impact	8
	2.3	The Problem of Comparing Apples to Oranges	12
3		**Experiments (A/B Testing)**	19
	3.1	Comparing Apples to Apples	19
	3.2	Behavioral Assumptions and Methods for Analyzing Experiments	22
	3.3	Multiple Interventions	26
	3.4	Use Cases in R	29
	3.5	Use Cases in Python	33
4		**Selection on Observables: Aim to Compare Apples with Apples**	37
	4.1	Making Groups Comparable in Observed Characteristics	37
	4.2	Behavioral Assumptions	41
	4.3	Methods for Impact Evaluation	42
	4.4	Use Cases in R	49
	4.5	Use Cases in Python	54
5		**Causal Machine Learning**	59
	5.1	Motivating Causal Machine Learning	59
	5.2	Elements of Causal Machine Learning	63
	5.3	A Brief Introduction to Several Machine Learning Algorithms	64
	5.4	Effect Heterogeneity and Optimal Policy Learning	69
	5.5	Use Cases in R	74
	5.6	Use Cases in Python	80
6		**Instrumental Variables**	87
	6.1	Instruments and Complier Effects	87
	6.2	Behavioral Assumptions and Methods	89

	6.3	Use Cases in R	93
	6.4	Use Cases in Python	96
7	**Regression Discontinuity Designs**	99
	7.1	Sharp and Fuzzy Regression Discontinuity Designs	99
	7.2	Behavioral Assumptions and Methods	102
	7.3	Use Cases in R	107
	7.4	Use Cases in Python	109
8	**Difference-in-Differences**	111
	8.1	Difference-in-Differences and the Impact in the Treatment Group	111
	8.2	Behavioral Assumptions and Extensions	114
	8.3	Use Cases in R	117
	8.4	Use Cases in Python	119
9	**Synthetic Controls**	123
	9.1	Impact Evaluation When a Single Unit Receives the Intervention	123
	9.2	Behavioral Assumptions and Variants	124
	9.3	Use Cases in R	128
	9.4	Use Cases in Python	131
10	**Conclusion**	133
	References	135
	Index	139

Preface and Acknowledgments

The datasets as well as the R and Python code considered in the use cases of this book are available on the Harvard Dataverse website "Data repository for 'Impact evaluation in firms and organizations'" at the URL https://doi.org/10.7910/DVN/2P8AY0.

The author is grateful to four referees for their valuable comments and suggestions, to Karin Lötscher for her assistance in designing several figures, to Lydia Dafflon for coding the use cases in Python, and to Sarina Joy Oberhänsli for her careful and thorough proofreading.

1 Introduction

Every day, companies and organizations face critical questions about the impact of their actions and interventions. Will increasing the price of a product or service affect sales? Can a marketing campaign increase customer retention? Does a training program for employees actually improve productivity? Will offering bonuses help retain employees? These are the kinds of pressing questions that decision-makers care about as they try to determine the best course of action to achieve their business goals. Therefore, answering such questions about causes and effects is fundamental for providing decision support on whether implementing or not implementing some intervention or policy (like a price increase, marketing campaign, employee training, or bonus payment) will likely pay off. In short, we are often interested in impact evaluation, that is assessing the impact of implementing (or not implementing) a specific intervention (like a marketing campaign) on a key performance indicator or outcome we care about (like sales). To do this, decision-makers frequently turn to quantitative approaches, using data-based methods to analyze real-world data (e.g., product, customer, and sales data) to gain insights into the causal relationships at play.

Despite the growing availability of data in the digital age, however, many companies still fail to use data-based methods like statistics or machine learning (a subfield of artificial intelligence) for impact evaluation in an appropriate way. Instead, firms tend to rely on such methods predominantly for a different task: forecasting (or prediction), which consists of accurately predicting a key performance indicator or outcome of interest, like sales, based on analyzing information in the data. More specifically, such predictive methods aim at understanding whether and how specific patterns in various characteristics (for instance, customers' income, age, or gender; product prices; or the day of the week) permit making educated guesses (or predictions) about an outcome like sales. In particular, machine learning algorithms (which are capable of learning autonomously from the data which characteristics are in which way relevant for making better predictions of the outcome) can be very effective. Indeed, in many domains, machine learning delivers better predictions than a human could ever make—provided that the information in the available data is sufficiently rich. It is therefore not surprising that the application of predictive methods (and machine learning in particular) has surged in many fields, such as marketing (e.g., sales forecasting), finance (e.g., prediction of stock price developments and other financial indicators), production (e.g., prediction of supply and prices of goods), and many more.

Given the wide success of quantitative methods for forecasting and prediction, one may feel tempted to directly apply them to impact evaluation, too. Unfortunately, it turns out that predictive methods are generally not suitable for providing answers to causal questions (which are essential for decisions on implementing interventions), a fact often overlooked by practitioners. For example, a predictive model might be able to predict customer churn (i.e., the likelihood that a customer will stop using our product or service), but it won't necessarily tell us which interventions are most effective for reducing churn overall or within different customer groups. Therefore, whenever data-based impact evaluation is the aim, analysts and decision-makers in companies and organizations should refrain from using predictive methods but, instead, need to turn to causal methods that have been developed exactly for the goal of answering cause-effect questions. However, discussions, sources, and use cases for the application of such causal methods in the business world are still rare.

This book aims to close this gap by providing a nontechnical introduction to methods for data-based impact evaluation in companies and organizations. It presents the most common quantitative methods for evaluating causal effects along with the statistical assumptions they rely on, which are, in fact, behavioral assumptions, that is assumptions about how humans behave. The book focuses on conveying the idea and intuition of the various evaluation approaches based on examples and graphical illustrations while keeping the formal discussion at a minimum. It targets a business audience (e.g., managers, executives, employees, IT specialists, and/or clerks) that is interested in obtaining a thorough understanding of the intuition, purpose, and practical implementation of impact evaluation, but without demanding a strong mathematical or quantitative background.

Impact evaluation has undergone a major transformation over the last few years, among them its combination with artificial intelligence (specifically, machine and deep learning) that appears very relevant in the light of the ongoing digitization and availability of more comprehensive data. In addition, we can observe a growing interest in companies and organizations for impact evaluation in order to provide evidence-based decision support. Among the leading users and developers of such methods are the big tech giants, who routinely run experiments on online market platforms to test the impact of their pricing policies and marketing strategies. In this book, not only do we discuss the methods, but we also provide a range of applications using the open-source software R and Python, which are very powerful tools for impact evaluation. This allows readers to immediately apply these methods of impact evaluation and causal machine learning based on user-friendly commands. The datasets as well as the R and Python code for the various use cases are available on the website "Data Repository for 'Impact Evaluation in Firms and Organizations'" at the URL https://doi.org/10.7910/DVN/2P8AY0.

The book starts with an introduction to the basics of impact evaluation in chapter 2, in particular, the concept of causality and the difference between the causal effect of an intervention on an outcome of interest and a mere noncausal association between the two. As an illustration, consider the case where customers possessing a loyalty card purchase on average more from the store issuing the loyalty card than those without loyalty card. It is a priori unclear whether this association actually corresponds to the causal impact of the loyalty card on purchases. It could, for instance, also be the case that the effect goes the other way round: those customers who purchase a lot get a loyalty card, so purchases affect the possession of a loyalty card, while the latter might have no impact on the purchasing volume.

Chapter 3 introduces the probably most intuitive impact evaluation method, the experiment, also known as A/B testing. This method randomly assigns the intervention whose impact is to be evaluated, such as an ad on an online market platform, implying that some customers coincidentally see the ad on the website, while others don't. In a properly conducted experiment, the customer groups receiving and not receiving the ad are comparable overall in terms of their background characteristics (like income or gender), due to the coincidental distribution of the ad. For this reason, differences in the outcomes across those groups (i.e., click rates or purchases on the website) plausibly reflect the causal impact of the ad, as it cannot be driven by differences in background characteristics.

Although experiments are often regarded as the gold standard for impact evaluation, there are many interesting questions in companies and organizations that cannot be answered using experiments. For this reason, the book also covers the most popular nonexperimental methods for assessing causal effects. Chapter 4 presents an approach based on the assumption that analysts can observe and measure all background characteristics that at the same time reflect the choice of the intervention, for example, receipt of a loyalty card, and the outcome, for example, purchasing behavior. These characteristics (also known as covariates) satisfying this behavioral assumption, which is known as the "selection-on-observables assumption," may, for instance, include age, income, or gender. The idea is to compare the purchases only of customers receiving and not receiving the loyalty card who are similar in terms of these characteristics. This ensures that we compare "apples with apples" when evaluating the impact of the loyalty card in order to avoid confusing its impact with any effects of (differences in) the characteristics. The aim is thus to mimic the experimental benchmark with the help of observed information. By finding customer groups with and without loyalty cards who are similar in observed characteristics, differences in the outcomes are assumed to be exclusively caused by differences in the intervention.

In light of the ongoing digitization and the ever-increasing availability of data and observed characteristics in many business domains, the question arises of how to optimally exploit this wealth of information for impact evaluation. To this end, chapter 5 combines the concepts of impact evaluation with a subfield of artificial intelligence, namely, machine learning. When relying on the selection-on-observables framework introduced in chapter 4, causal machine learning algorithms can learn in a data-driven way which characteristics importantly influence the intervention and the outcome, ensuring that we compare apples with apples. This becomes particularly relevant in big data contexts, where the number of observed characteristics is vast.

Another important domain of causal machine learning is data-driven detection of significant differences in impact across subgroups or customer segments. For example, a marketing intervention may be more successful in promoting a product among younger customers than among older ones, implying that the impact of marketing varies (or is heterogeneous) across age groups. Causal machine learning algorithms can learn in a data-driven way which characteristics (like age) importantly drive the size and heterogeneity of the impact, which can, for instance, be useful for customer segmentation. Very closely related to this argument is a another variant of causal machine learning called optimal policy learning. It aims at the marketing campaign optimally targeting specific subgroups or customer segments defined in terms of observed characteristics (e.g., younger or older customers) by the marketing campaign to maximize its effectiveness.

Chapter 6 introduces an evaluation approach based on so-called instruments, which are characteristics that affect the intervention whose impact is of interest but do not directly affect the outcome. This is easiest described in the context of a broken (i.e., failed) experiment, in which some subjects deviate from their assigned intervention. Imagine an experiment conducted by a company that randomly (i.e., coincidentally) invites or encourages customers to attend a promotion event, but some invitees decide to not participate. While the invitation is random and therefore satisfies the experimental context, the decision to participate is not. Those customers not participating despite being invited might, for instance, be less interested than others in the company's services or products.

In this case, the interest levels of participants and nonparticipants (rather than invited and not invited customers) differ, such that comparing the outcomes, for example, purchasing behavior, of both groups would mix up the impact of the event with that caused by differences in interest. In this context, the invitation may be used as an instrument if it induces at least some customers to participate in the event but does not directly affect the purchasing behavior other than through event participation. This seems plausible if the invitation per se does not, for instance, affect the preferences for the company's products or services. In this case, we can adjust (or scale) the impact of the invitation on the purchasing behavior by the impact of the invitation on event participation, to ultimately obtain a measure of the impact of event participation on purchasing behavior.

Chapter 7 delves into "regression discontinuity designs" (RDDs), which aim to mimic the experimental context of a randomly (or coincidentally) assigned intervention based on an index (or so-called running variable), which determines access to the intervention. More concisely, if that index reaches or is above a certain threshold value, then the intervention is granted, while for index values below the threshold, this is not the case. To better illustrate this concept, let's consider an internet provider that computes for each customer a score for how likely it is that the customer will switch to a different provider, a behavior known as customer churn. This score may come from a statistical model that factors in a customer's past internet usage, income, and other relevant factors. To retain customers, the internet provider offers a discount to any customer whose index (or likelihood to switch) exceeds a certain threshold. Similar to an experiment, customers slightly above and slightly below this threshold are arguably quite comparable, as their index value differs only slightly. At the same time, those slightly above the threshold receive the discount, while those slightly below do not. By comparing comparable customers above and below the threshold in terms of their outcomes, like customer retention, the RDD evaluates the impact of the discount.

Chapter 8 explains the "difference-in-differences" (DiD) approach for impact evaluation. We can apply this approach if the outcome of interest is observed over time, that is, prior to and after the introduction of an intervention, and if the intervention is introduced only to one group but not to another. The method presumes that the outcomes of both groups (with and without intervention) would have experienced the same change over time (i.e., would have followed a common trend) in the absence of the intervention. As an example, consider a training on workplace health promotion as an intervention, which is introduced in some, but not all, departments of a company or organization. The management is interested in the training's impact on workplace-related accidents.

Simply comparing the number of accidents of employees with and without training does not necessarily inform the company about the effect of the training program, because the departments offering and not offering the training might systematically differ in terms of background characteristics (like the structure of jobs and tasks) that matter for the likelihood of accidents. Comparing accidents before and after the introduction in departments offering the training will not be informative either if there is a general time trend in accidents even in the absence of any intervention, for example, due to a growing health awareness among employees over time. However, if this time trend in health awareness is common, that is, comparable in all departments, we can easily measure it in those departments that do not introduce the training. By comparing the change in accidents in departments offering the training before and after the introduction (which consists of both the training's impact and the trend) to the corresponding change in departments not introducing the training, we ultimately obtain the impact of the training.

Chapter 9 presents the "synthetic control" method, another evaluation approach for outcomes observed prior to and after the introduction of an intervention. It is particularly suitable for case study setups where only one subject receives the intervention and several others do not. The method assesses the impact by comparing the outcome of the reference subject that receives the intervention to a weighted average of outcomes of subjects without the intervention. Therefore, the weighted average serves as a "synthetic" imputation of what the outcome of the reference subject would have looked like in the absence of the intervention. The importance (or weight) any subject without the intervention obtains in the computation of that average depends on how similar it is to the reference subject (receiving the intervention) prior to the intervention in terms of observed outcomes (and possibly also background characteristics).

Therefore, the behavioral assumption is that an appropriate mix of subjects that entails outcomes (and characteristics) similar to those of the reference subject in the periods prior to the intervention makes it possible to assess its impact after its introduction. As an example, consider a reference production site that introduces a new production technology, while other sites do not. To evaluate the impact of the technology on productivity, we first appropriately mix the sites not introducing the technology to generate a synthetic site that resembles the reference site in terms of the productivity prior to the introduction of the technology. Second, we evaluate the impact as the divergence in productivity of the reference and the synthetic site after the introduction of the technology.

Finally, chapter 10 concludes the book and provides a brief discussion of recent developments in business-related impact evaluation for decision support.

2 Basics of Impact Evaluation

2.1 The Fundamental Problem of Impact Evaluation

In the realm of impact evaluation, the focus is on assessing how a specific intervention within a company or organization influences a desired outcome, typically represented by measures of success like key performance indicators (KPIs). The definition of such outcomes should be guided by the core business objectives and goals, taking considerations like risk tolerance or financial stability into account. These objectives may encompass aspirations for growth, such as expanding market share or venturing into new markets, or profit-oriented aims such as increasing profitability, enhancing margins, or streamlining cost efficiency. For instance, pertinent business outcomes could revolve around metrics like market share or sales per customer.

The challenge of determining the causes of and effects on such outcomes stems from the fact that at any moment, we cannot observe the world with and without the intervention we aim to evaluate at the same time. To give an example, let's imagine we want to evaluate the impact of a marketing campaign on the sales of a product or service in different stores. To assess the effectiveness of the marketing campaign, we would ideally love to compare sales that would have been realized in any store when running versus not running the campaign. However, the harsh reality is that a store can either run the campaign or not, but not both at the same time. This makes it impossible to observe the same store under two mutually exclusive scenarios—that is, marketing versus no marketing—and therefore, we cannot directly observe the impact of the campaign for any store. This is known as the "fundamental problem of causal inference" (or impact evaluation), as discussed in Holland (1986).

As a further decision problem, suppose a company wants to evaluate the impact of a new pricing strategy on sales of a particular product. The new strategy involves offering a discount to customers who purchase the product in combination with another product, with the goal of increasing overall sales. However, it is impossible to observe the sales of the same customer in both the discounted and nondiscounted scenarios at the same time. Therefore, the company cannot directly observe the causal effect of the pricing strategy on sales. Another example from the business world that illustrates the fundamental problem of causal inference is the evaluation of employee training programs. Companies often invest substantial resources in providing training programs to their employees, with the goal of improving their productivity and job performance. To assess the impact of the training program, we would like to compare the productivity of each employee when receiving versus not receiving the training. However, as we cannot simultaneously observe an employee with and without the training, we cannot directly observe the impact of the training program on each individual employee, which poses a challenge for evaluating the effectiveness of the program.

Despite the fundamental problem of causal inference, we might still be able to assess the impact of an intervention, under the condition that we can make specific assumptions about human behavior that appear plausible in our context and apply causal methods that rely on these behavioral assumptions. By gaining an understanding of these methods and the related behavioral assumptions, and by learning how to implement them in statistical software like R and Python, we can overcome the fundamental problem of causal inference. This book is designed to provide you with the tools and knowledge to do just that. Whether you're interested in evaluating the effectiveness of a marketing campaign, pricing strategy, or employee training program, this book will help you navigate the complex world of impact evaluation with confidence. So, let's dive in and uncover the secrets of causal inference.

2.2 Characterizing the Impact

Although this book aims to avoid formal (mathematical or statistical) notation, we will from time to time make use of letters to represent particular phenomena, which we call variables. These variables may, for instance, correspond to the intervention (like a marketing campaign) whose impact is of interest or the outcome (like sales), the key performance indicator on which the impact should be assessed. The purpose of using different letters to refer to different variables is to appropriately define and describe the impact of interest. Let's denote the intervention as D, which could represent a marketing campaign, price dicount, or some other action taken in a company or organization. Importantly, D can take different values depending on whether the intervention is introduced or not. When assessing a marketing campaign, the intervention indicates whether a store runs the marketing campaign or not. So, if $D=1$, it means that a store is running a marketing campaign, while $D=0$ means that it is not. Furthermore, we denote by Y the outcome based on which the effect of the intervention should be assessed. Y could stand for sales, number of store visits, net benefits, or other key performance indicators. For instance, if a store made a turnover of $30,000 on a specific day, we can say that $Y = 30,000$.

Using this letter notation, we can characterize and investigate the impact of the marketing campaign intervention D on sales Y. Figure 2.1 provides a graphical representation of the impact we are interested in, which is given by the causal arrow going from the campaign intervention D to the sales outcome Y. Such causal graphs offer an intuitive way of displaying causal relations between different variables, as discussed in Pearl (2000). In figure 2.2,

Basics of Impact Evaluation

Figure 2.1
Impact of intervention (D) on outcome (Y)

Figure 2.2
Impact of a marketing intervention on sales outcome

the same graphical representation is provided without using the letters D and Y to represent the intervention and outcome. Instead, the campaign intervention and sales outcome are directly named. Both figures convey the same information, but the use of letters offers a more versatile approach. It allows the definition of intervention and outcome to adapt based on the specific context of interest. For example, in scenarios involving HR policies rather than marketing campaigns, D might represent employee training instead of a marketing intervention, while Y might indicate employee productivity rather than sales outcomes.

Rather than using causal graphs as in figures 2.1 and 2.2, we may also exclusively rely on letter notation to define the impact of interest. Intuitively, the sales impact of the marketing campaign corresponds to the difference in a store's sales outcome that would potentially be realized with the campaign (when $D=1$) versus without it (when $D=0$). Therefore, we can represent a store's potential sales outcome with and without the campaign using $Y(1)$ and $Y(0)$, respectively. The impact of the campaign is simply the difference between these potential outcomes—that is $Y(1) - Y(0)$. For example, suppose a store would have made sales of \$30,000 when running a campaign ($Y(1) = 30,000$) but only \$20,000 when not running the campaign ($Y(0) = 20,000$). In that case, the impact of the campaign would be $Y(1) - Y(0) = 10,000$. This is illustrated in the bar chart provided in figure 2.3, where the bars represent the potential outcomes with the intervention, $Y(1)$, and without the intervention, $Y(0)$, and the difference between them corresponds to the impact. However, this effect cannot be directly observed if one of the potential outcomes is unknown.

Indeed, the use of this potential outcome notation, as advocated by Neyman (1923) and Rubin (1974), not only provides a clear way to define causal effects but also makes it possible to highlight the previously mentioned fundamental problem of causal inference: that is, the observed sales outcome Y alone does not reveal the causal effect $Y(1) - Y(0)$ without further action from an analyst or researcher. This is because, for stores that run the marketing campaign ($D=1$), the observed sales Y correspond to the potential sales with the campaign, $Y(1)$. However, the potential sales outcome without the campaign, $Y(0)$, is unknown for those stores, such that we cannot measure the impact $Y(1) - Y(0)$. Similarly, for those stores not running the campaign ($D=0$), the observed outcome Y equals $Y(0)$, while $Y(1)$ remains

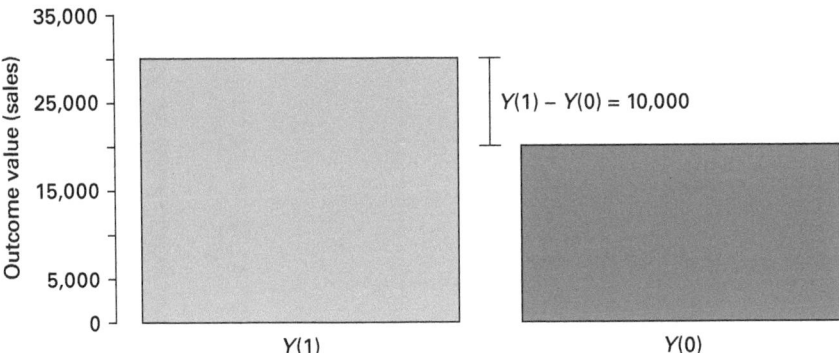

Figure 2.3
Potential outcomes and impact

unknown. Therefore, the relationship between the observed and potential outcomes can be described as follows:
$$Y = Y(1) \text{ if } D = 1, \quad Y = Y(0) \text{ if } D = 0. \tag{2.1}$$

As potential outcomes $Y(1)$ and $Y(0)$ are never observed simultaneously for any store, the impact of the intervention $Y(1) - Y(0)$ cannot be calculated straightforwardly, posing a fundamental problem of causal inference. However, this problem can be overcome under certain behavioral assumptions using certain methods, as we will discuss later in this book.

One important behavioral assumption inherent in our definition of potential outcomes $Y(1)$ and $Y(0)$, as well as the impact $Y(1) - Y(0)$, is that a store's sales outcome is influenced solely by the marketing intervention in that store, without being affected by interventions in other stores. In other words, customers' buying behavior in a store is assumed to be independent of whether a marketing campaign is introduced in another store. If this were not the case, we would need to consider potential sales outcomes based not only on the campaign in the store of interest but also on campaigns in other stores. This consideration would account for spillover (or interference) effects, where customers, for example, may see a product ad in a different store and decide to purchase that product in our store, even though our store did not advertise it. For this reason, spillover effects may not only benefit the store implementing the intervention but also impact competitors within the same market or industry in both the short and the longer run, for instance, through downstream impacts on brand perception or customer trust. However, incorporating such spillover effects complicates impact evaluation in terms of notation and methods. Hence, in the ensuing discussion, we will adhere to the assumption of no spillover effects, a behavioral assumption known as the "stable unit treatment value assumption" (SUTVA) [see, for instance, the discussion in Rubin (1980) and Cox (1958)].

Basics of Impact Evaluation

Although we cannot directly observe causal effects for any subject like individual stores or customers, there are certain assumptions, such as the SUTVA, that allow us to evaluate them on a more aggregate level—that is, based on groups of units exposed and not exposed to the intervention. One effect that is of particular interest is the average causal effect. This is the average impact among all subjects in a predefined population, such as the average impact of the marketing campaign on sales in all stores or the average impact of a discount on the purchasing decision of all customers. We denote this average causal effect by Δ, which is formally defined as the average difference in potential outcomes (like potential sales) with and without intervention (e.g., with and without a marketing campaign):

$$\Delta = E[Y(1) - Y(0)]. \tag{2.2}$$

The expression '$E[\ ]$' in equation (2.2) stands for "expectation," which is simply the average in the population of interest (like all stores or all customers in a country or market). To illustrate, consider a population of only two stores, where the marketing campaign has no effect on sales in the first store but increases sales by $20,000 in the second store. In this case, the average causal effect is $10,000. In real-world examples, we are, however, often interested in the average impact on considerably more subjects. The average causal effect is also frequently referred to as the average treatment effect and is commonly abbreviated as ATE, as an intervention is often also called a treatment, in particular, in medical trials conducted, for example, by the pharmaceutical industry to assess the effectiveness of new medical treatments.

Rather than looking at the average causal effect for the entire population, we might be more interested in the impact of the intervention on a specific group, in particular, the subpopulation that actually received the intervention. For example, we might want to learn the average impact of the marketing intervention only among those stores that actually run the campaign and not among those that do not—for example, because it is not planned to roll out the campaign to all stores. This subpopulation receiving the intervention (or treatment) is known as the treatment group, and the average impact in in this group is called the average treatment effect on the treated (abbreviated as ATET or ATT), which we denote by $\Delta_{D=1}$. It is formally defined as

$$\Delta_{D=1} = E[Y(1) - Y(0)|D=1], \tag{2.3}$$

where $|D=1$ is to be read as "only for those who actually received the intervention," or "conditional on the receiving intervention." That is, '$|$' is to be understood as "condition," meaning that this average effect only concerns the subpopulation satisfying the condition of $D=1$, receiving the intervention. Analogously, we may also consider the average impact in the population not receiving the intervention, for example, the average sales effect of the marketing campaign in stores not running the campaign. This effect is relevant for the decision of whether the campaign should be rolled out to additional stores and is known as the average treatment effect on the nontreated (ATENT)—that is, on those not receiving the intervention. We denote the ATET by $\Delta_{D=0}$, which is formally defined as follows:

$$\Delta_{D=0} = E[Y(1) - Y(0)|D=0]. \tag{2.4}$$

2.3 The Problem of Comparing Apples to Oranges

After having defined aggregate causal effects like the ATE and the ATET, a natural question is how to properly assess them. Would it be appropriate to compare the average outcomes of units receiving the intervention or treatment (like customers receiving a discount), commonly referred to as the "treatment group," the with those not receiving the intervention (customers not receiving any discount), the "control group"? Unfortunately, it's not that simple in most cases, as this approach only works if the treatment and control groups are comparable in terms of background characteristics that affect the outcome. In practice, however, the treatment and control groups frequently differ in background characteristics. This implies that the average differences in the outcomes between treatment and control groups not only reflect the impact of the intervention but might also be driven by differences in the background characteristics.

Let's take the example of a shop that issues loyalty cards to its customers, which give access to certain benefits like reduced prices when a certain minimum amount of purchases is surpassed. The management wants to know if the loyalty card intervention increases the volume of purchases, which is the outcome of interest. However, customers who obtain a loyalty card might purchase more than those who aren't interested in the loyalty card, even if no card is issued to anyone. This is because customers who regularly shop at the store see the benefit of getting a loyalty card, while those who do not regularly shop at the store get lower or no benefits from holding a loyalty card. Therefore, customers with and without loyalty cards differ in terms of their buying intent.

For this reason, simply comparing the average purchases of loyalty cardholders and nonholders does not inform us about the impact of the loyalty card intervention on purchases, as this approach mixes the effect of the loyalty card with that of the differences in buying intent. Put differently, by comparing loyalty cardholders with nonholders, we compare apples with oranges, as the two groups differ in an important background characteristic that also affects purchases, namely buying intent. The difference in average outcomes therefore also reflects differences in the buying intent, and not (only) the effect of the loyalty card. We could, for instance, find a positive difference, meaning that cardholders buy more than nonholders, even when there is no impact of the loyalty card whatsoever.

As another example, consider the issue of customer churn, meaning that customers change their service provider, for example, their internet, mobile phone, or health insurance provider. To prevent customers from leaving, providers might offer discounts to incentivize them to stay. But does offering a discount actually work? That's the question on the mind of a provider, who is interested in whether the discount has a positive effect on customer retention, meaning that such a price intervention reduces customer churn. However, there is a catch: the provider might give the discount only to customers deemed to have a high churn intention, meaning they are at a high risk of leaving. So simply comparing the churn rate of customers who received the discount (the treatment group) versus those who did not (the control group) will not give us an accurate picture of the discount's impact, because the two groups differ in terms of their churn intention. It is like comparing apples with oranges, so we cannot separate the effect of the discount from the effect of differential churn intentions. For example, we may see no difference in retention rates between the two groups and wrongly conclude that the discount had no effect. In reality, the discount may have been successful in increasing retention, but its positive effect was offset by the higher churn intention of the customers who received it, such that the discount's impact is masked by comparing apples with oranges.

The problem of having treatment and control groups with different background characteristics, such as buying intent, that affect the outcome, such as purchases, is known as selection bias. This means that the two group are "selective"—that is, different from each other, just as apples are different from oranges. In terms of our notation, this implies that the difference in the average of the observed outcome Y in the treatment group $D=1$ and the average of Y in the control group with $D=0$ does not necessarily correspond to the impact of intervention D. Based on a causal graph, we can characterize the selection problem visually. To this end, we modify the causal graph from figure 2.1 in chapter 2, section 2.2 by adding the letter U, which represents one or even multiple background characteristics (such as buying intent, income, and gender).

Selection bias, or the apples and oranges problem, arises if U affects both the intervention D (such that treatment and control groups differ in U; e.g., holders and nonholders of loyalty cards have different buying intent) and outcome Y (buying intent affects actual purchases). This is represented by the causal arrows going from U to D and from U to Y, respectively, in figure 2.4. The arrows are dotted (rather than solid) to indicate that such characteristics U are frequently not observed in the data, making it impossible to assess their causal effect on D and Y. Thus, whenever it is plausible that there are characteristics that jointly affect the intervention and the outcome, we cannot easily assess the impact of the intervention by naively comparing the outcomes of the treatment and control groups. In figure 2.5, an equivalent graphical representation is provided without using the letters D, Y, and U to represent the intervention and outcome but by directly naming the loyalty card as the intervention, purchases as the outcome, and buying intent as one possible unobserved characteristic affecting both the receipt of a loyalty card and the purchasing behavior, although there might be many more such characteristics in practice.

To properly evaluate the impact of an intervention D, such as a loyalty card, on an outcome Y, like purchases, the treated and control groups must be comparable in terms of any background characteristics U, like buying intent, that affect outcome Y. In statistics this

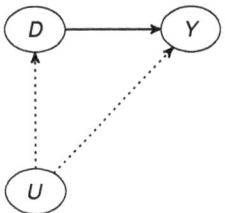

Figure 2.4
Selection bias

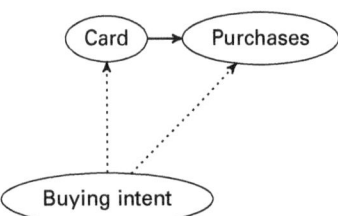

Figure 2.5
Selection bias when evaluating a loyalty card

is known as the "ceteris paribus" condition, meaning "everything else equal" apart from the intervention. Visually, this means that if U affects Y, it must not affect D, as displayed in figure 2.6. For instance, if buying intent affects purchases, it must not also influence the decision to obtain a loyalty card, in order to satisfy the (ceteris paribus) condition that buying intent does not systematically differ across the treatment and control groups. Only then can we attribute any differences in average purchasing outcomes Y across the treated and control groups to the intervention alone, rather than the background characteristics. In this case, we can determine the average impact of the intervention (or ATE) without interference (or confounding) by the background characteristics, which would jeopardize our impact evaluation.

Let's dive into the issue of selection bias in a more formal manner. We can denote the average outcome in the treatment group as $E[Y|D=1]$ (recalling that "$|D=1$" indicates "among those with $D=1$") and the average outcome in the control group as $E[Y|D=0]$. If $E[Y|D=1] - E[Y|D=0]$ is different from zero (such that holders and nonholders of loyalty cards differ in average purchases), then we say that Y and D are correlated. However, a correlation between intervention D and outcome Y does not necessarily imply a causal effect of D on Y, a point made by Haavelmo (1943), among many others. It is interesting to note that the absence of correlation—that is, $E[Y|D=1] - E[Y|D=0] = 0$—does not necessarily imply no causation either. It could just happen that the effect of the intervention D and

Basics of Impact Evaluation

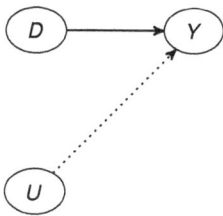

Figure 2.6
No selection bias

the selection bias due to the background characteristics cancel each other exactly out (e.g., with the effect of D being positive and the selection bias being negative). In such a case, we could have $E[Y|D=1] - E[Y|D=0] = 0$ despite the intervention having a nonzero effect. In summary, when we have apples and oranges due to selection bias, the difference in average outcomes between the treatment and control groups does not inform us about the impact of the intervention. Using our potential outcome notation, we can formalize this insight by stating that the presence of selection bias means that

$$E[Y|D=1] - E[Y|D=0] \neq \underbrace{E[Y(1) - Y(0)]}_{\Delta}. \qquad (2.5)$$

Figure 2.7 visually demonstrates the issue of incomparability between treatment and control groups in terms of background characteristics. In this representation, figures of the same color represent subjects with shared characteristics, such as buying intent or income, whereas figures of different colors represent subjects with differing characteristics that influence outcomes, such as purchasing behavior. With the treatment group ($D=1$) comprising three black figures and one white figure, and the control group ($D=0$) consisting of one black and three white figures, the two groups are not comparable. Consequently, comparing or taking the difference in the average outcomes of the treatment and control groups does not correspond to the ATE.

Only in the absence of selection bias, as in the scenario shown in figure 2.6, does the difference in average outcomes of the treatment and control groups corresponds to the average impact of the intervention (ATE):

$$E[Y|D=1] - E[Y|D=0] = \underbrace{E[Y(1) - Y(0)]}_{\Delta}. \qquad (2.6)$$

The difference in average outcomes across the treatment and control groups, $E[Y|D=1] - E[Y|D=0]$, corresponds to the ATE Δ because both groups are representative of each other and of the entire population in terms of background characteristics U. Therefore, we compare apples to apples.

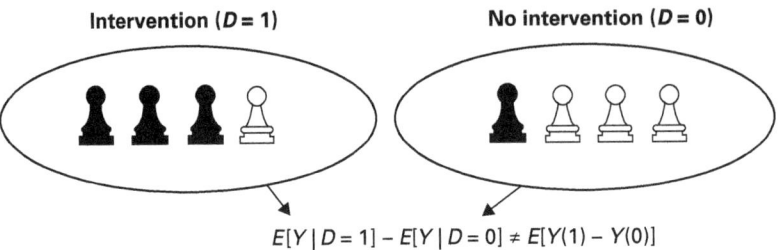

Figure 2.7
Incomparable treatment and control groups

Indeed, the difference in average outcomes across groups generally only corresponds to the ATE if the following conditions are met. First, the average outcome (e.g., average purchases) in the treatment group (receiving the loyalty card) is representative of the potential purchases that would on average have occurred in the entire population if everyone had received a loyalty card. Second, the average purchases in the control group (not receiving the loyalty card) are representative of the potential purchases that would on average have occurred in the entire population if nobody had received a loyalty card. These conditions rule out that any background characteristics U (like buying intent) affecting the purchases outcome are on average different across the treatment group, the control group, or the entire population (which consists of both the treatment and control groups). To sum up, treatment and control groups must be representative of the whole population in terms of U (or at least average values of U) to satisfy equation (2.6) and rule out selection bias, as illustrated in figure 2.6.

Conversely, if this condition is not met, then U affects both D and Y, leading to selection bias. In this case, we should refer to figure 2.4 and equation (2.5) instead of figure 2.6 and equation (2.6), which means that we cannot confidently infer causality from average outcome differences. Unfortunately, we cannot directly observe the existence and magnitude of selection bias in the data, just like we cannot directly observe causal effects. The reason for this is that we cannot observe the average potential outcomes in the whole population, $E[Y(1)]$ and $E[Y(0)]$, as we only know either $Y(1)$ or $Y(0)$ for any individual. Therefore, we cannot verify whether equation (2.6) is true, which would imply comparing apples to apples (meaning that the treatment and control groups are representative of each other and the entire population). Therefore, it is typically difficult to ascertain whether and to what extent selection bias affects a given dataset.

In general, we would suspect selection bias to be an issue in most data that we observe, because people tend to act in a strategic way based on their personal characteristics. For instance, in our example of the loyalty card, it seems probable that individuals with a stronger inclination to buy would more often opt for the card, while those with lower buying intent (and lower benefits to be expected from holding such a card) might not. In the upcoming chapters, we will explore various alternative methods that can still measure the impact of an intervention if we can make specific assumptions about how humans behave in certain contexts. These methods vary in terms of the behavioral assumptions (often referred to as "identifying assumptions") they rely on for measuring (or identifying) the impact of the intervention. As these assumptions often are not verifiable (or testable) in the data, it's crucial to thoroughly examine whether they are likely to hold or not in the data to be analyzed, for example, by relying on theoretical reasoning or previous empirical evidence.

3 Experiments (A/B Testing)

3.1 Comparing Apples to Apples

Experiments, also known as A/B testing, have been considered one of the most intuitive and, if properly conducted, most credible methods to impact evaluation, and they date back (at least) to Fisher (1935). They have found frequent application in marketing research, such as assessing the impact of coupons for specific goods or services, as demonstrated by Bawa and Shoemaker (1989), or analyzing discount schemes, as seen in the study by Fong et al. (2015). Experiments consist of "coincidentally" (or randomly) granting or denying access to some intervention (for instance, a price discount or an ad campaign), like a coin flip. Therefore, the participants of the treatment and control groups are chosen exclusively by "luck" (like the result of the coin flip) rather than based on their background characteristics. Graphically, random assignment of the intervention corresponds to the framework in figure 2.6 in chapter 2, where background characteristics, denoted by U, do not affect the intervention, denoted by D, because D is exclusively determined by the coin flip.

The randomness of the selection process ensures that the background characteristics of the participants in each group are comparable, at least when the number of participants in the experiment is sufficiently large. This means that we can measure the impact of the intervention by simply comparing the outcomes (e.g., purchasing behavior) of the treatment and control groups, as there are no systematic differences in other characteristics (e.g., income, gender, buying inclination) that could also influence the outcome. This concept is illustrated in figure 3.1, where figures of the same color represent subjects with shared background characteristics, while figures of different colors represent subjects with differing characteristics. Since both the treatment ($D=1$) and control ($D=0$) groups comprise two black and two white figures, the two groups are comparable. Consequently, the difference in the average outcomes of the treatment and control groups corresponds to the intervention's average treatment effect (ATE).

One example of A/B testing in the business world is how e-commerce websites test different versions of their website to see which design elements lead to increased sales or click-through rates. For example, a company could run an experiment to compare the

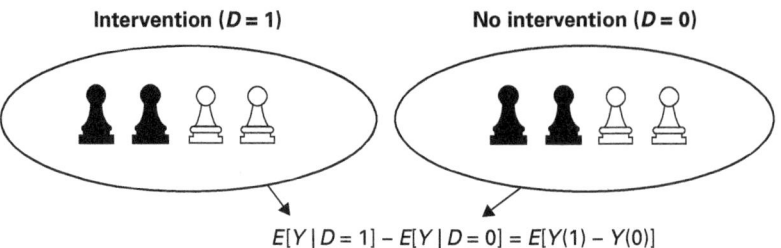

Figure 3.1
Comparable treatment and control groups

performance of two versions of the product page: the control version, which is the original page, and the treatment version, which is the modified version. In the treatment version, the website owner may choose to make changes such as adding more product images, improving the product description, changing the color scheme, or altering the placement and color of the "buy" button. Similarly, a company could evaluate the impact of alternative versions of online ads on conversion outcomes like purchases, page views, and downloads; see Gordon et al. (2022) for an example.

Furthermore, a streaming service (for films or series) may use A/B testing to evaluate the impact of different recommendation algorithms on user engagement and content consumption. For instance, the platform could run an experiment where one group of users is exposed to the existing recommendation algorithm (control group), while another group experiences a modified version of the algorithm (treatment group). The modified algorithm might prioritize personalized recommendations based on genres or actors the user has previously watched, while the existing one follows a different set of criteria. By analyzing metrics such as time spent on the platform, click-through rates, or user ratings between the two groups, the streaming service can determine which algorithm generates more engagement and user satisfaction, in order to increase user retention.

But A/B testing is not limited to online businesses and can also be used in offline settings. For instance, a brick-and-mortar store might use A/B testing to evaluate the effectiveness of different store layouts or product displays. Imagine a grocery store that wants to determine whether placing a particular product at the end of an aisle (i.e., "end cap") will increase sales compared to placing the same product on a regular shelf. The store could randomly assign different locations to the product for a period of time and compare the sales figures between the two groups. By doing so, the store can determine whether the end cap placement is more effective in increasing sales and adjust its store layout accordingly.

Furthermore, a retail chain might employ A/B testing to assess the impact of in-store promotions on customer purchases. For instance, a clothing store could run an experiment to compare two different promotion strategies for a specific clothing line. The control group

Experiments (A/B Testing)

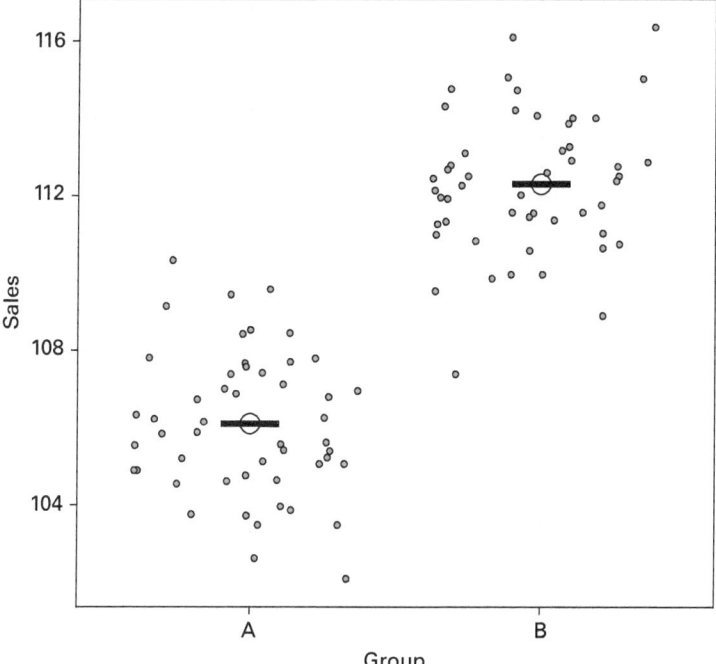

Figure 3.2
A/B testing

might receive traditional discount coupons via mail, while the treatment group gets notified about a special in-store event featuring the clothing line with personalized styling sessions. By tracking the sales and foot traffic between the two groups during the promotional period, the store can gauge which approach drives higher sales and customer engagement. This information helps the retailer understand which promotional strategy is more effective in attracting customers and increasing purchases, guiding future marketing campaigns and in-store events.

Figure 3.2 illustrates the use of A/B testing for evaluating the impact of an intervention like an ad campaign. In this example, group A has not been exposed to the campaign, while group B has. To assess the campaign's impact, we compare the individual sales (which is our outcome of interest) in groups A and B. The individual sales for each member of the two groups are represented by the dots on the y-axis, while the x-axis represents the two groups. The larger points with bars show the average sales for each group. We see that average sales are higher in group B, which has been exposed to the campaign, than in group A. Therefore, our experiment indicates a positive impact of the ad campaign on average sales.

3.2 Behavioral Assumptions and Methods for Analyzing Experiments

In the following, we provide a more formal discussion of the behavioral assumptions underlying experiments, or A/B testing. Random assignment of the intervention D ensures that subjects with specific background characteristics U, such as high or low values, are equally likely to receive or not receive the intervention. Consequently, the treatment and control groups are comparable in terms of characteristics U and, hence, the potential outcomes $Y(1)$ and $Y(0)$ that they would realize with and without intervention. This comparability follows because the background characteristics U are the only factors that influence the outcome Y besides the intervention D, as illustrated in figure 2.6. In statistical terms, we say that D is statistically independent of $\{Y(1), Y(0)\}$ if $Y(1)$ and $Y(0)$ are comparable across groups with and without intervention due to their comparability in U.

Formally, this statistical independence can be expressed as follows:

$$\{Y(1), Y(0)\} \perp D, \tag{3.1}$$

where '$\perp$' denotes statistical independence. Because potential outcomes are comparable across treatment and control groups, experiments are not susceptible to the selection bias problem discussed in chapter 2, section 2.3. Therefore, both groups are representative of the population in terms of background characteristics. In other words, comparing treatment and controls groups is comparing apples with apples. For this reason, the difference in the average outcomes of the treated and control groups correspond to the ATE (as stated in equation (2.6) in chapter 2, section 2.3) in experiments with properly randomized interventions that meet the independence assumption in expression (3.1).

Regarding the practical implementation of experiments, it is important to keep in mind that the average difference $E[Y|D=1] - E[Y|D=0]$ and the ATE Δ defined in equation (2.2) pertain to the entire population. This includes, for instance, all customers in a given region or market. However, in reality, experiments are usually conducted on a limited number of participants who are to be randomly drawn from the population of interest. For instance, we might coincidentally or randomly select 10,000 customers in a region, which (by random selection) should be representative of the total of customers in that region in terms of background characteristics (like buying intent). These 10,000 customers form our sample for evaluating the impact of our intervention. To do this, we randomly assign the intervention (e.g., a discount) to, for example, 5,000 customers in our sample while withholding it from the remaining 5,000. Finally, we measure the average outcome in the treatment and control groups and calculate the difference to assess the average treatment effect. Suppose we find that average sales in the treatment group amount to $20,000, while those in the control group are $15,000. This yields an ATE of $20,000 - 15,000 = \$5,000$ in our sample.

To distinguish between the impact estimated in the sample and the true impact in the population, we use a "hat" symbol, $\hat{}$, for any parameter calculated in the sample. For instance,

$\hat{E}[Y|D=1]$ and $\hat{E}[Y|D=0]$ indicate the average outcomes among the treatment and control groups of 5,000 customers each. The difference between the two provides the sample-based ATE estimate, denoted by $\hat{\Delta}$:

$$\hat{E}[Y|D=1] - \hat{E}[Y|D=0] = \hat{\Delta}. \tag{3.2}$$

However, it is important to note that the sample-based ATE estimate $\hat{\Delta}$ may not exactly match the true ATE Δ in the population of interest. For instance, it may happen that our sample is not fully representative of the entire population, because we might by chance have selected a somewhat higher share of customers with specific background characteristics (like a higher buying intent) to participate in our sample than is prevalent in the population. Such issues can, for instance, arise if the data used for the experiment are outdated and no longer accurately reflect the current composition of the population. Furthermore, it may happen that within our sample, the customers we randomly assign to the treatment and control groups might not be fully comparable either.

For instance, the share of females might by chance be slightly higher in the treatment than in the control group. However, if we are successful in randomly recruiting participants from the population and randomly assigning the intervention in our evaluation sample, these issues of noncomparability tend to be small or even close to nonexistent if our sample is sufficiently large. By analyzing large enough samples to ensure a high level of representativeness between the sample and population, we can expect the ATE estimate $\hat{\Delta}$ to be reasonably close to the true ATE Δ. Indeed, the more participants we have, the greater are the chances that $\hat{\Delta}$ will be very close to Δ, in line with a statistical rule known as the "law of large numbers."

One convenient way of analyzing the difference in the average outcomes of the treatment and control groups in the sample as considered in equation (3.2) is a statistical technique called linear regression. It was first suggested by Gauss (1809) and is one of the most popular techniques for quantitative analysis. When applied to an experiment, linear regression provides us with two statistical parameters called "coefficients." The first coefficient measures the average outcome in the control group of our sample, $\hat{E}[Y|D=0]$. The second coefficient represents the difference in the average outcomes between the treatment and control groups in our sample and therefore the estimated ATE, $\hat{E}[Y|D=1] - \hat{E}[Y|D=0] = \hat{\Delta}$. To formally set up a linear regression equation that characterizes the average outcome based on these coefficients and the intervention, let's denote the two coefficients by α and β and mark them with a hat symbol, $\hat{}$, to indicate that they come from a sample (rather than the population).

The linear regression equation is given by

$$\hat{E}[Y|D] = \underbrace{\hat{E}[Y|D=0]}_{\hat{\alpha}} + \underbrace{(\hat{E}[Y|D=1] - \hat{E}[Y|D=0])}_{\hat{\beta}} \cdot D, \tag{3.3}$$

where $\hat{E}[Y|D]$ denotes the average outcome in a specific group in our sample, depending on which value D takes. For $D=1$, this corresponds to the average outcome in the treatment

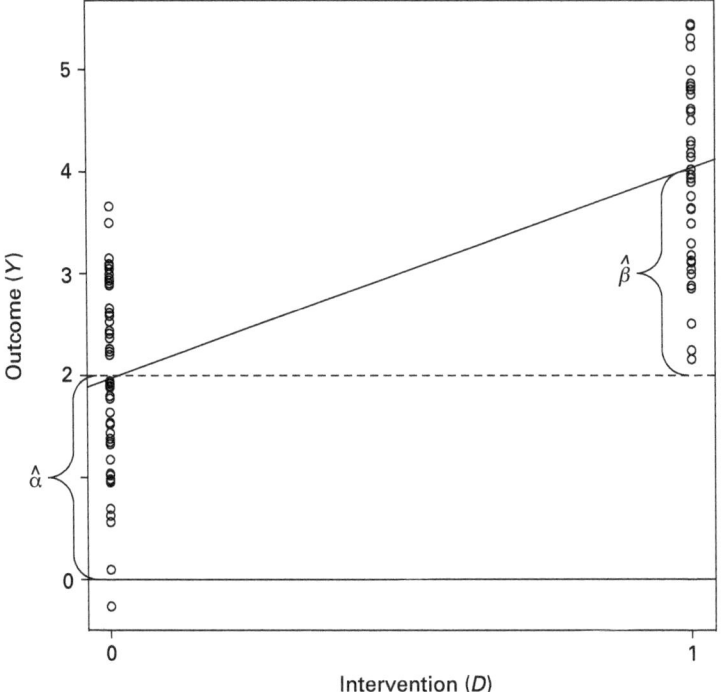

Figure 3.3
Linear regression

group in our sample, while for $D=0$, we obtain the average outcome in the control group. The crux of this discussion is that by using linear regression, we can calculate a coefficient, denoted by $\hat{\beta}$, that represents the estimated ATE, which is the impact we are interested in. Additionally, linear regression also gives us the average outcome without the intervention, which is represented by $\hat{\alpha}$.

The intuition of linear regression is illustrated graphically in figure 3.3. The dots in the plot represent the subjects in our data, such as customers. For each customer, we observe the outcome Y (e.g., customer satisfaction measured by an index on a scale of 0 to 8), which is plotted on the y-axis. On the x-axis, we have the intervention D (e.g., a communication campaign) that each customer receives, which can be either 0 or 1. The solid regression line shows how the average outcome changes across values of the intervention. $\hat{\alpha}$ corresponds to the average outcome in the absence of the intervention, also visualized by the dashed line, which is 2 in our example. On the other hand, $\hat{\beta}$ corresponds to the difference in the average outcome between customers who received the intervention and those who did not, which is the estimated impact.

As we have discussed earlier, estimating the ATE from a sample may not always be fully accurate, as the sample or the treatment and control groups may not by fully representative of the population. Regression techniques provide us not only with the estimated impact but also with a measure of uncertainty, namely the variance, that we face when estimating the impact in a sample. A low variance indicates that we have a good chance that the impact measured in our sample comes close to the true impact in the population. Conversely, a high variance points to a high risk of obtaining an impact that is substantially different from the true effect. Therefore, it is crucial to assess the variance to determine how confident we can be in the impact measured in our sample. This permits considering the following interesting question (among others): What is the probability of observing an impact as large in absolute magnitude as estimated in my data, $\hat{\beta}$, or even more extreme (further from zero), if the true ATE in the population (β) is actually zero? This probability, known as the p-value, measures how unusual the impact observed in the data would be if the true ATE was zero. For example, a p-value of 5% means that if there were no impact in the population, the probability of estimating an impact as extreme as the one obtained in the sample, $\hat{\beta}$, or even more extreme is just 5%, under the given variance of the estimation method. Like all probabilities, a p-value falls within the range of 0% and 100%.

The p-value is different from, but linked to another crucial question: What is the probability of making an error when asserting that the true impact in the population differs from zero, based on the observed impact in my sample? Put differently, what is the chance of incorrectly claiming that there is a nonzero impact in the population, given the results in the sample? This probability is known as the type I error probability. In impact evaluations, analysts typically define a maximum acceptable type I error probability for claiming an impact, referred to as the significance level. For instance, setting the significance level at 5% implies that the risk of the true effect in the population being zero, despite a nonzero impact in the sample, should not exceed 5%. While p-values and type I error probabilities are different concepts, it is noteworthy that when the p-value is lower than a chosen significance level, such as 5%, we reject the idea or hypothesis of no impact in the population (and claim the impact to be non-zero) with the understanding that the probability of a type I error (incorrectly claiming an impact) does not exceed 5%. Comparing the p-value to the significance level thus allows us to decide whether to claim a non-zero impact in the population or not.

Another useful application related to measuring the variance (or uncertainty) of the estimated impact is computing a range, or interval, of values that contain the true impact in the population with a certain likelihood or probability (when running the analysis in many samples). These intervals are called confidence intervals, and they allow us to assert with a certain level of confidence that the true effect lies within the interval. For example, suppose we estimate the sales effect of a marketing intervention to be $20,000 based on our sample. In light of the variance of the estimated impact, we may find with 95% probability that the true effect in the population lies anywhere between $10,000 and $30,000. It is worth noting that the sample size plays a crucial role for the variance and the width of the confidence interval. If we increase the number of participants in our experiment, we decrease the level of uncertainty, or variance, in the impact evaluation. This is because we base our analysis on more observations, which also narrows the confidence interval. For instance, suppose we consider a sample of 4,000 participants instead of only 1,000. In that case, the 95% confidence interval may range from $15,000 to $25,000, rather than $10,000 to $30,000.

3.3 Multiple Interventions

In the previous chapters, we focused on the impact of a single intervention. However, in real-world scenarios, we are often interested in comparing the effectiveness of multiple interventions that may be competing with each other. Take the example of an online platform that is considering different advertising campaigns on its website, such as various versions of an online ad or different locations of an ad on the website. In such a case, the platform management might want to know the impact of each campaign on the click rates, which refer to how often internet users click on an ad to obtain more product information. To measure the impact, we can conduct an experiment where we randomly assign different campaigns to different internet users who visit the website, while some users do not receive any ad at all. By comparing the average click rates of the group exposed to a specific campaign (e.g., a flashy ad in the upper-right corner of the screen) to the control group not receiving any ad, we can estimate the average impact of that campaign. We can repeat these pairwise comparisons with the control group for each advertising campaign to identify the most effective ad. For instance, our analysis might reveal that a flashy ad placed in the upper-right corner of the screen leads to a higher click rate than a neutral ad in the lower-left corner.

Experiments could also be used for analyzing different doses or intensities of an intervention. Take, for example, a train company looking to boost sales by offering discounts on off-peak train rides. The company might be unsure how much of a discount is needed to incentivize customers to purchase more tickets. Perhaps a discount of 10% is enough to increase sales, but would a larger discount of 40% lead to even more sales? To answer this question, the train company could conduct an experiment where they randomly offer different discount levels to customers and then compare the number of tickets sold under each discount. By using experiments to analyze the relative impact of different discount doses, the train company can make informed decisions about how much of a discount to offer that balances financial feasibility with increased sales.

In experiments with enough doses, we can even assess the impact of small or marginal changes in the intervention—for example, the effect of increasing the discount from 4% to 5% or from 14% to 15%. To analyze such marginal effects across different values of the intervention, we can again rely on regression techniques. However, using linear regression with an intervention taking many values (also called a "continuously distributed" intervention) assumes that increasing the intervention always has the same marginal effect. This

Experiments (A/B Testing)

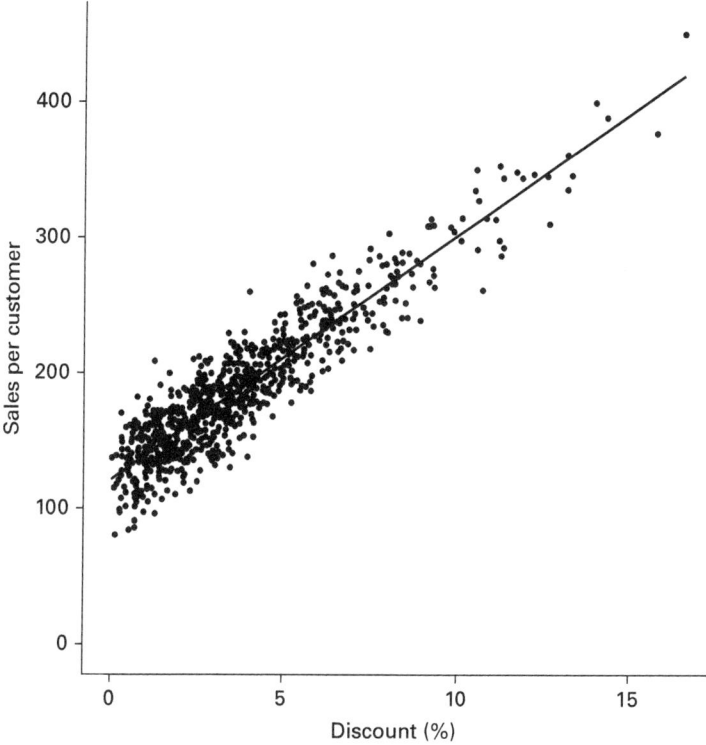

Figure 3.4
Average outcomes under homogeneous impacts

assumption implies that marginally increasing the discount from 4% to 5% has the same impact on a sales outcome as marginally increasing the discount from 14% to 15%. In this case, we say that the impact of the intervention is homogeneous—that is, it does not depend on the initial value of the discount before increasing it.

This implies that there is a linear association between the outcome and the intervention, as shown in figure 3.4. The dots in the plot represent specific subjects, such as customers. For each customer, the outcome (e.g., sales per customer) is plotted on the y-axis, while the intervention (e.g., the discount received by the customer) is plotted on the x-axis. The solid line represents the association between the average outcome and the intervention, which is linear since the impact of the intervention is homogeneous. This means that increasing the intervention by one percentage point has the same effect regardless of the initial value of the discount.

While linear regression is suitable for evaluating an intervention that only takes the values 1 or 0 (e.g., a marketing campaign) as discussed in section 3.2, or an intervention with many values that has a homogeneous impact, it is generally inappropriate in other scenarios.

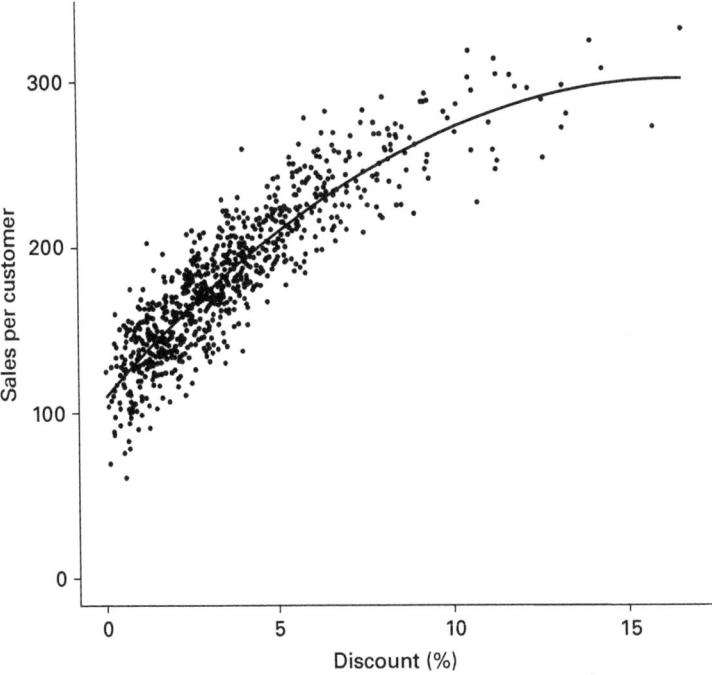

Figure 3.5
Average outcomes under heterogeneous impacts

Ideally, we would like to use a method that allows marginal effects to vary across different values of the intervention, as it is not guaranteed that the intervention always has the same impact. For instance, we want to allow for the possibility that increasing a discount from 4% to 5% may have a different impact on sales than increasing it from 14% to 15%, as there is no reason to believe that a 1% increase has the same effect across all discount margins.

Figure 3.5 illustrates a scenario where the impact of the intervention varies across different levels of the intervention, meaning that the impact is hetergeneous (rather than homogeneous). The y-axis shows the outcome, which is sales per customer, while the x-axis represents the intervention, namely the discount measured in percentage points. The dots in the graph represent the sales and discounts of specific customers. The solid line shows the association between average sales per customer and the discount level—that is, the average outcome across different values of the intervention. We observe that among customers with relatively small discounts (e.g., 4%), an increase in the discount has a noticeable effect in terms of extra sales created, as the solid line is clearly upward sloping for low values of the intervention. However, for comparatively high values of the discount (e.g., 14%), increasing the discount has a relatively small effect, as the solid line demonstrating the association between sales and discounts is rather flat for such values of the intervention.

We note that so-called nonparametric (rather than linear) regression techniques are capable of flexibly assessing the impact of marginal changes in the intervention across different values it takes—for example, for discounts ranging from 0% to 20%, given that the sample contains enough observations (as the method is relatively data hungry). Intuitively, nonparametric methods measure average outcomes among participants whose intervention values are equal or sufficiently close to the intervention value of interest to assess the impact of a marginal increase in the intervention. For example, suppose we are interested in a discount of 10%. In that case, we can consider the average outcome of all customers receiving discounts in the range of 9% to 11% and give more importance (or weight) to those with a discount of exactly 10% when computing that average. We can then see how much the average outcome changes when we slightly increase the discount value of interest to 11%, computed based on all customers with discounts between 10% and 12%. This approach, using "moving" averages to compute average outcomes and marginal changes, is known as kernel regression, which is one example of a flexible method for assessing marginal effects of interventions that take many values. The original proposal for kernel regression dates back to the work of Nadaraya (1964) and Watson (1964).

3.4 Use Cases in R

Now it is time to put into practice what we have learned in the previous chapters. Let's dive into a real-world use case of an experiment and see how we can analyze it. We'll be focusing on an information intervention that was randomly assigned, and we'll be using the statistical software R to perform our analysis. We will estimate the average impact of the intervention based on the difference in average outcomes between treatment and control groups ($\hat{\Delta}$). The intervention was conducted by the nongovernmental organization Ecosystem Europe and involved the random distribution of leaflets containing information about the environmental and social implications of coffee production among high school and university students in Bulgaria. Some students received the leaflets, while others did not. In a subsequent survey, all students were asked to participate, and their awareness of environmental issues related to coffee production was measured.

Our objective is to evaluate the impact of the leaflet on one of these awareness outcomes, specifically awareness of waste production due to coffee production, using R. To this end, we first use the *install.packages* command to install three packages that contain the dataset and specific R commands useful for our analysis: the *causalweight* package includes the *coffeeleaflet* data with 522 observations on Bulgarian students, while the *lmtest* and *sandwich* packages include procedures for impact evaluation based on regression as discussed in section 3.2. We install these three packages by running the code *install.packages(c("causalweight", "lmtest", "sandwich"))*. Once the packages are installed, we load them into the R workspace using the *library* command, for example, by running *library(causalweight)* to load the *causalweight* package. Next, we load the *coffeeleaflet* dataset into the R workspace using the *data* command, for example, *data(coffeeleaflet)*. The dataset consists of 48 variables, including the intervention named *treatment*, which is 1 if a student received the leaflet and 0 if not, and the outcome variable *awarewaste*, which measures a student's awareness of waste production due to coffee production on a five-point scale (1 = not aware, ... , 5 = fully aware).

To assess the average impact, also known as the average treatment effect (ATE), we run a linear regression using the *lm* command. In this command, we have to specify the outcome, in our case *awarewaste*, and the intervention, *treatment*, and separate the former from the latter by the expression ∼ (tilde): *lm(awarewaste~treatment)*. As we want to save the results of our analysis, we generate a new object in our R workspace, which we name *results*, and define it to correspond to the regression output using the equals sign (=): *results=lm(awarewaste treatment, data=coffeeleaflet)*. Finally, we apply the command *coeftest(results, vcov=vcovHC)* to display the results of our analysis stored in the object *results*. The box below provides the R code for each of the steps:

```
install.packages(c("causalweight","lmtest","sandwich"))   # install packages
library(causalweight)                                     # load causalweight package
library(lmtest)                                           # load lmtest package
library(sandwich)                                         # load sandwich package
data(coffeeleaflet)                                       # load coffeeleaflet data
results=lm(awarewaste~treatment, data=coffeeleaflet)      # estimate impact
coeftest(results, vcov=vcovHC)                            # show impact
```

Running this code yields the following output:

```
             Estimate  Std. Error  t value   Pr(>|t|)
(Intercept)  2.007874   0.062992   31.8752  < 2.2e-16  ***
treatment    0.280126   0.094466    2.9654   0.003167  **
---
Signif. codes:  0 '***' 0.001 '**' 0.01 '*' 0.05 '.' 0.1 ' ' 1
```

The first column (*Estimate*) yields the coefficient estimates. The first row *(Intercept)* corresponds to the average outcome in the control group, $\hat{E}[Y|D=0]$. The result thus suggests that the average awareness among those not receiving the intervention is roughly 2.01 points on a five-point scale (1 = not aware, . . . , 5 = fully aware). The second row *(Treatment)* provides the average impact of the intervention, $\hat{\Delta}$. Our analysis suggests that the information leaflet increases the awareness of coffee-induced waste production on average by 0.28 points, from 2.01 points without intervention to 2.29 points with intervention. The fourth column *(Pr(> |t|))* contains the *p*-values related to our estimates, the probability of finding an average effect as large as 0.28 points, or even further from zero, in our sample if there is actually no effect in the population. For the average impact of the intervention, $\hat{\Delta}$, the *p*-value is just 0.003 (or 0.3%).

Therefore, we can with high confidence reject the possibility (or hypothesis) that the intervention has an average impact of zero in the population. This is because the *p*-value is substantially lower than any conventional significance level that sets the maximum acceptable error probability of incorrectly asserting a nonzero effect in the population based on the results in our sample, such as 5% or 1%. This statistical significance is also indicated by the two stars, **, implying statistical significance at the 0.01 (or 1%) level according to the significance codes (*Signif. codes*). This is the statistical parlance for saying that in light of our estimated nonzero effect, the chance that the true average impact is actually zero in the population from which we have drawn our database is below 1%.

As a second use case, we consider an example of an intervention with many doses. To do this, we install and load the *datarium* package by Kassambara (2019), which contains the *marketing* dataset, and the *np* package by Hayfield and Racine (2008) for kernel regression using the *install.packages* and *library* commands. Next, we load the *marketing* data by using the *data* command. The data contain 200 observations with information on sales and advertising budgets, including a variable called *newspaper* that measures the budget of advertisement in newspapers, measured in thousands of dollars. The newspaper budget is our intervention, which was presumably randomly assigned to experimentally assess the impact on the *sales* of a product, which is the outcome measured in thousands of product units sold.

We use the *npregbw* command for kernel regression to estimate how the average of *sales* changes across different budget values of *newspaper* by putting the expression *sales* ~ *newspaper* into the command. As the second argument in the *npregbw* procedure (which is separated by a comma from the first one), we define *data* = *marketing* to indicate that the *npregbw* command should select the *sales* and *newspaper* variables from the *marketing* dataset when running the analysis. We store the results of the analysis in an R object named *results* by using the equals sign: *results* = *npregbw(sales* ~ *newspaper, data* = *marketing)*. To graphically display the association between average sales and the newspaper advertising budget, we apply the *plot* command. The first argument of the latter is *results*. As the second argument (separated from the first one by a comma), we specify *plot.errors.method* = *"asymptotic"*, which also plots the confidence intervals that cover the true effect with a probability of 95%. The box below provides the R code for the various steps:

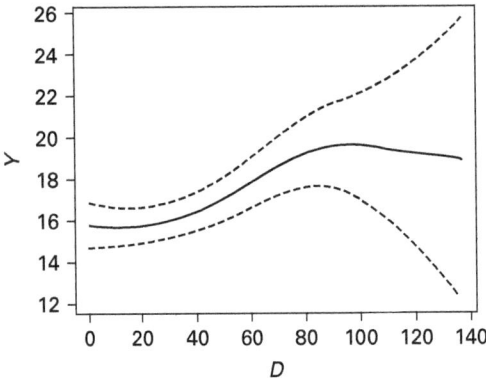

Figure 3.6
Estimation of the conditional mean outcome

```
install.packages(c("datarium", "np"))              # install packages
library(datarium)                                   # load datarium package
library(np)                                         # load np package
data(marketing)                                     # load marketing data
results=npregbw(sales~newspaper, data=marketing)    # kernel regression
plot(results, plot.errors.method="asymptotic")      # plot average sales
plot(results, gradients=TRUE, plot.errors.method="asymptotic") # plot effects
```

Running the code yields the graph in figure 3.6. The y-axis in the latter gives the average sales, while the x-axis provides the values of the advertising budgets (in thousands of dollars). By and large, the (solid) line suggests that newspaper advertisement positively affects average sales up to a budget of roughly $90,000, while the association is rather flat (and even slightly decreasing) for even higher budgets. However, it needs to be pointed out that the association between average sales and advertising budgets is not estimated with very high confidence for larger values of the advertising intervention, as the (dashed) confidence intervals become very large beyond budgets of $90,000. Due to this wide range of values within the intervals, the method is not very precise in pinning down what the association between sales and newspaper advertising actually is for budgets higher than $90,000. This is due to the small number of observations with such high spending on advertising. For lower budget values, however, we not only find a positive association but also have narrower confidence intervals. This implies that we have more confidence that the association between sales and advertising for lower budgets is also positive in the entire population (e.g., a market), not just in our sample.

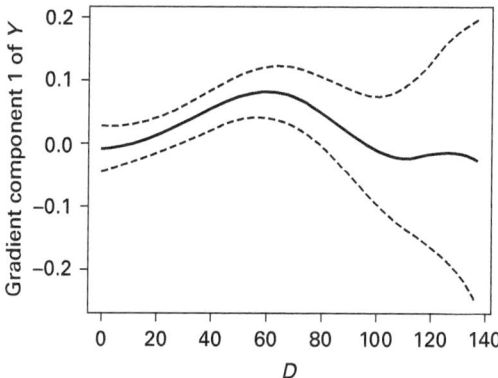

Figure 3.7
Estimation of the marginal effects

The *np* package also allows us to plot the marginal effects of a budget increase on average sales, which is the change in average sales due to a slight increase in the advertising budget. Mathematically, this corresponds to the first derivative of the plot in figure 3.6. To plot the marginal effects, we add the argument *gradients=TRUE* to the previous *plot* command (again, separated from previous arguments by a comma):

```
plot(results, gradients=TRUE, plot.errors.method="asymptotic") # plot effects
```

Running the code produces the graph shown in figure 3.7. The graph shows that the marginal effects of a slight increase in the advertising budget on average sales are positive, with high statistical confidence, over a limited range of budget values around $60,000. Specifically, the (dashed) 95% confidence intervals do not include a zero impact within this range. In these cases, the *p*-value is less than 5%. This means that the effects are statistically significant at the 5% significance level, which by convention allows us to claim that the error probability of incorrectly assuming a nonzero impact in the population does not exceed 5%. On the other hand, when considering larger values of the intervention, the marginal effects are statistically insignificant at the 5% significance level. This is because the 95% confidence intervals are quite wide and always include a zero impact.

3.5 Use Cases in Python

This section presents the Python implementation for the two use cases discussed in the previous section 3.4, which used R for conducting the analysis. The datasets considered below and in all remaining Python use cases in the book are available in csv (comma-separated values) format on the website "Data Repository for Impact Evaluation in Firms and Organizations" at the URL https://doi.org/10.7910/DVN/2P8AY0. The first use case aims at assessing the impact of an information intervention on the awareness of waste production due to coffee cultivation. We initiate the process by importing the Python libraries *pandas* for data manipulation and *statsmodels* for statistical modeling. Then, we load the *coffeeleaflet.csv* dataset into a Pandas dataframe named *df* using the *read_csv* function. In the next step, we retain only the relevant intervention and outcome variables (*treatment* and *awarewaste*) using the *loc* function. We handle missing observations by dropping them from the dataset using the *dropna()* command.

Next, we define the intervention D to correspond to the variable *treatment* and add a constant term (a column of ones) to D using the command *sm.add_constant(D)* (to obtain an intercept in the linear regression to be conducted). Furthermore, we define the outcome Y to correspond to the variable *awarewaste*. We then estimate the ATE of the treatment on the outcome by linear regression, using the command *OLS(Y, D).fit(cov_type ='HC0')* from the *statsmodels* library and save the output in a Python object named *results*. Finally, we apply the *print* command to display the regression output, which is stored in the object *results.summary()*. The box below provides the Python code for the various steps, which yields exactly the same impact of a 0.28-point increase in awareness of waste production as found in the R-based analysis in the previous section:

```
import pandas as pd                                    # load pandas library
import statsmodels.api as sm                           # load statsmodels library
df = pd.read_csv('data/coffeeleaflet.csv')             # load coffeeleaflet data
df = df.loc[:, ['treatment', 'awarewaste']]            # only keep columns of interest
df = df.dropna()                                       # drop missing observations
D = df['treatment']                                    # define treatment
D = sm.add_constant(D)                                 # add a constant
Y = df['awarewaste']                                   # define outcome
results = sm.OLS(Y, D).fit(cov_type = 'HC0')           # estimate impact
print(results.summary())                               # show results
```

Let's now consider the second use case discussed in the previous section 3.4, which involves assessing the impact of an advertising intervention with multiple doses on product sales. We first import several Python libraries: *pandas* for data manipulation, *numpy* for numerical operations, *statsmodels* for statistical modeling, and *matplotlib* for plotting. We

Experiments (A/B Testing)

then load the *marketing.csv* dataset into a Pandas dataframe named *df* using the *read_csv* function. Next, we define the outcome variable *Y* to correspond to product sales and the intervention *D* to correspond to the advertising budget in newspapers. We define the range of values of the intervention at which the analysis should be conducted to be within the minimum and maximum value of the intervention *D*, using the *x_axis* command. We then perform a kernel regression of the outcome *Y* on the treatment *D* using the *KernelReg* function. We plot the average sales against the advertising budget using the *plot* function, and then plot the marginal effects using the same *plot* function. The two plots provide a graphical representation of the association between the advertising budget and product sales, as well as the marginal effects of changes in the advertising budget on average sales in a similar way as figures 3.6 and 3.7 did for the R-based implementation. The box below provides the Python code for the various steps:

```python
import pandas as pd                              # load pandas library
import numpy as np                               # load numpy library
import statsmodels.api as sm                     # load statsmodels library
import matplotlib.pyplot as plt                  # load matplotlib library
df = pd.read_csv('data/marketing.csv')           # load marketing data
Y = df['sales']                                  # define outcome
D = df['newspaper']                              # define treatment
x_axis = np.arange(min(D), max(D))               # define points where we evaluate
results = sm.nonparametric.KernelReg(Y,D,'c', reg_type='lc').fit(x_axis) #kernel
plt.plot(x_axis, results[0], color='black')      # plot average sales
plt.xlabel('newspaper')                          # label x axis
plt.ylabel('sales')                              # label y axis
plt.ylim([12, 26])                               # setting y-axis range
plt.show()                                       # show the plot
plt.plot(x_axis, results[1], color='black')      # plot impact
plt.xlabel('newspaper')                          # label x axis
plt.ylabel('marginal effects')                   # label y axis
plt.show()                                       # show the plot
```

4 Selection on Observables: Aim to Compare Apples with Apples

4.1 Making Groups Comparable in Observed Characteristics

Companies and organizations often face significant challenges when attempting to conduct experiments, such as A/B tests, to address their causal inquiries. For example, A/B testing typically assesses short-term effects, which may fail to capture the long-term impact of interventions such as pricing changes on outcomes such as customer behavior and brand perception. Furthermore, experiment results may suffer from sampling bias, where participants do not adequately represent the broader population, such as the entire customer base. Another issue is that experiments often have limited scope, focusing on specific changes, such as minor pricing adjustments, without considering a broader range of factors that may causally affect outcomes like customer behavior. Indeed, for many interesting interventions, it might be impractical or impossible to assess their impact due to financial or organizational constraints. For instance, it might not be deemed justifiable to manipulate product quality in an experiment to investigate customer response.

For these reasons, many impact evaluations are based on so-called observational (rather than experimental) data, which may come from surveys (e.g., an online survey among customers), company data (e.g., product features and sales in stores), or administrative data (e.g., information on demographic characteristics of a country or region). Observational data typically encompass not only the intervention under evaluation and its associated outcomes but also further observed variables known as covariates. These covariates might include details about a customer's age, gender, income, or past purchasing behavior. However, unlike experimental data, interventions are typically not randomly assigned in observational data. Therefore, simply comparing the average outcomes of treatment and control groups is insufficient for evaluating the intervention's impact, an issue that comes on top of other possible challenges like the previously mentioned sampling bias.

Nevertheless, there are scenarios where meaningful causal analysis can be conducted with observational data, even in the absence of experimental design. This is possible if we can leverage the covariates to ensure comparability between treatment and control groups in all characteristics that influence both the intervention and the outcome. In other words, by only

Figure 4.1
Comparing apples with apples

comparing the outcomes of treatment and control groups with the same or at least very similar covariates, we aim at comparing apples with apples, as required for a proper impact evaluation. This concept is illustrated in figure 4.1, where figures of the same color represent subjects with comparable covariates, while figures of different colors represent subjects with differing covariates. As the treatment group comprises three black figures and one white figure, and the control group ($D = 0$) consists of one black and three white figures, it is evident that the two groups are not directly comparable. However, by selectively comparing subsets of figures across the treatment and control groups that share the same color, we aim to evaluate the intervention's impact within subsets that are comparable in terms of covariates.

Indeed, we hope (rather than know) that making treatment and control groups comparable with respect to covariates is sufficient, but we can never be certain that the two groups do not also differ in other outcome-relevant characteristics that we cannot observe. For example, imagine we want to evaluate the impact of a loyalty card on purchases and compare customer groups holding and not holding a card that are comparable in covariates like education, gender, and age. However, we cannot be certain that these covariates account for all differences in buying intent between the two groups. If this is not the case, then the two groups differ not just in terms of covariates but also in unobserved characteristics, like certain personality traits, that affect the outcome (purchases). In such a scenario, our aim of comparing apples with apples did not (fully) succeed. We ended up comparing apples with oranges due differences in unobserved characteristics that entail differences in the outcome that cannot be attributed to the intervention. Therefore, exploiting covariates for impact evaluation relies on the behavioral assumption that the information in these covariates is rich enough to generate treatment and control groups that are comparable just like in an experiment, which is known as the "selection-on-observables" assumption. Put differently, the assumption implies that the intervention is as good as being randomly assigned among subjects that are comparable in terms of their covariates.

Let's for instance consider the impact of a discount on customers' buying decisions in an online marketplace. The selection-on-observables assumption implies that when only considering customers who are comparable in covariates like past buying behavior, which may affect both current purchases and the likelihood of being offered a discount, receiving a discount or not is as good as random. This assumption may be plausible if the characteristics

Selection on Observables: Aim to Compare Apples with Apples

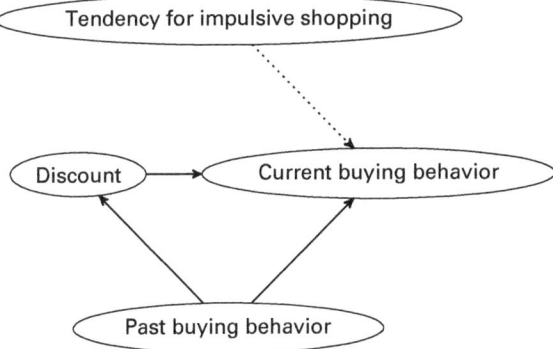

Figure 4.2
Selection on observables when evaluating a discount

that importantly influence the discount are well known and observed in the data, such as if the online marketplace offers discounts based on a customer's past purchasing behavior. Additionally, unobserved characteristics that affect the outcome should be unlikely to also affect the discount after accounting for the covariates to make our assumption plausible. This condition is met, for example, when particular customer characteristics affecting current purchasing behavior—such as a tendency for impulsive shopping—have no relevance concerning the receipt or nonreceipt of a discount.

When finding comparable treatment and control groups in terms of observed characteristics, it is important to measure these characteristics prior to the intervention. If we measure them after, the measured characteristics may have been affected by the intervention, such that any differences in postintervention characteristics between the treatment and control groups may reflect part of the intervention's impact, rather than preexisting differences. Clearly, differences in the buying behavior of customers who received a discount and those who did not may be due to the discount's impact. Therefore, we want to compare groups with similar buying histories before the discount (to compare apples with apples), while any difference after the discount could indicate the presence of an impact. As this impact is what we want to evaluate, we would not want to make the groups comparable in their buying behavior after the intervention took place, as doing so would incorrectly skew (or bias, to use statistical parlance) the impact.

Figure 4.2 illustrates our scenario of selection on observables using a causal graph, where causal effects are depicted by arrows. The focal causal effect we aim to measure is the impact of the discount on a customer's current buying behavior, our outcome variable. This is complicated by the fact that a customer's past buying behavior influences both the receipt of a discount and the current buying behavior, such that we need to find discount recipients and nonrecipients who are comparable in their past buying behavior before evaluating the discount effect. Besides past buying behavior, a customer's tendency for impulsive shopping also affects current buying behavior but does not influence discount receipt. Therefore, if this causal model is correct; it is not problematic if we lack a measure of a customer's tendency for impulsive shopping in our data (which is illustrated by the dotted causal arrow, indicating the unobserved nature of the tendency for impulsive shopping). However, apart from past buying behavior, there might still be other characteristics influencing both discount receipt and current buying behavior. For a sound causal analysis, we would need to find groups of discount recipients and nonrecipients that are comparable in these characteristics, too.

It is worth noting that in many contexts, the selection-on-observables assumption is unlikely to be met. Often, we do not have access to all the information necessary to plausibly reflect all the factors that affect both the intervention and the outcome. For example, imagine a company introducing employee training on IT tools to improve productivity. Employees with specific personality traits such as high levels of motivation may be more likely to participate in such a training than others, while at the same time also being more productive. This makes it difficult to attribute the training's impact solely to the intervention. To address this, we should compare the productivity of groups with and without training who are similar in terms of their motivation levels and other relevant personality traits. Unfortunately, information on these traits (like motivation, intelligence, self-confidence, and others) is often unavailable in datasets. In this case, making treatment and control groups comparable based solely on observed characteristics will still entail a comparison of apples with oranges. Therefore, we need to scrutinize the plausibility of the selection-on-observables assumption based on domain knowledge, intuition, or insights from previous analyses, which can guide us in identifying which characteristics likely affect both the intervention and the outcome.

As a practical example of a possible failure of the selection-on-observables assumption, Gordon et al. (2022) evaluated the effects of online ads on conversion outcomes (e.g., purchases, page views, and downloads) on a social media platform using data from 663 experiments involving approximately 7.9 billion user observations and over 38 billion ad impressions. They contrasted these experimental effects with analyses of observational (nonexperimental) online data based on the selection-on-observables assumption. To measure the impacts in the observational data, the authors utilized a comprehensive set of covariates, including user characteristics, estimated intervention-specific conversion probabilities, and preintervention outcome variables. If the selection-on-observables assumption was valid, meaning that all factors jointly influencing ad assignments and outcomes were adequately considered, the estimated impacts should closely mirror the experimental effects (assuming proper experimental conduct). However, findings from Gordon et al. (2022) point to a substantial overestimation of the ads' impact in observational data relative to the experimental results. In subsequent chapters, we will explore alternative causal strategies that can be employed when the selection-on-observables assumption fails, while still leveraging other (potentially equally stringent) behavioral assumptions to facilitate a meaningful evaluation of the intervention's impact.

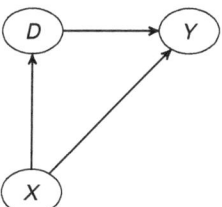

Figure 4.3
Selection on observables

4.2 Behavioral Assumptions

To visually represent the selection-on-observables assumption in a general way, let X represent the observed characteristics (like past purchases, gender, or income), also known as covariates, in the dataset. Figure 4.3 displays a causal graph that satisfies our assumptions. The covariates X jointly affect the intervention D (like a discount) and the outcome Y (like present buying behavior), and given X (i.e., for subjects with the same covariates), there are no additional, unobserved variables that influence both D and Y. This still allows for sets of unobserved variables that affect D or Y separately, but these sets (which are not shown in the graph) must not be associated (e.g., correlated) with each other.

We note that, in addition to the selection-on-observables assumption, there is a second condition that needs to be met. Specifically, for each value of the characteristics occurring in the treatment group, there must exist subjects with comparable values of these characteristics in the control group, and vice versa. For example, if we want to compare the productivity of employees who received training with those who did not, and we consider age to be an important characteristic, then we must ensure that there are employees of comparable age in both groups. If some employees in the treatment group are 35 years old, then there must also be individuals in the control group with a comparable age so that we can make an apples-to-apples comparison. This condition of having comparable subjects in both groups for all possible values of the observed characteristics is known as "common support." If this condition is not met, then we cannot evaluate the impact of the intervention because there are no comparable units in the treatment and control groups. For instance, if there are no employees in the control group with a comparable age to some employees in the treatment group, then it becomes impossible to make a direct comparison of the productivity between trained and untrained employees within that specific age group.

In addition to the graphical approach, we can formalize the selection-on-observables assumption using the potential outcome framework discussed in chapter 2, section 2.2. The assumption can be expressed as follows:

$$\{Y(1), Y(0)\} \perp D | X. \tag{4.1}$$

Expression (4.1) indicates that if we consider only units with identical values of X (see "$|X$"), the treatment is equivalent to being randomly assigned. This can be understood by noticing that the first part of expression (4.1) without "$|X$"—namely, "$Y(1), Y(0) \perp D$"—is identical to expression (3.1) in chapter 3. In addition to the selection-on-observables assumption, we can also formalize the common support assumption. For an intervention that can only take the values 1 (e.g., discount) and 0 (no discount), it corresponds to

$$0\% < \Pr(D=1|X) < 100\%. \tag{4.2}$$

$\Pr(D=1|X)$ is the probability of obtaining the intervention among subjects with specific values of covariates X (e.g., age $= 35$). This represents the proportion of subjects with those covariate values who receive the intervention (e.g., 60% of those aged 35 receive the training). This share must be larger than 0% and smaller than 100%, implying that there are both subjects who receive the intervention and those who do not for all values of the covariate X in the population of interest.

In the selection-on-observables framework, the treatment and control groups may differ in terms of their covariates X. As a result, the impact may also vary if it depends on the covariates. For instance, the impact of a discount may vary across different buying behaviors. The discount might be more or less effective in increasing purchasing behavior among previously frequent buyers than less frequent buyers. In contrast to experiments, where randomization ensures that the treatment and control groups have comparable characteristics (including covariates X), it may be useful to explore effects for specific subpopulations defined in terms of whether they receive the intervention. For example, it may be interesting to examine the effects on individuals in the treatment group, who actually receive the intervention. This suggests that, in addition to the average treatment effect (ATE) for the entire population, we may also be interested in the average treatment effect on the treated (ATET), as discussed at the end of section 2.2.

4.3 Methods for Impact Evaluation

In our selection-on-observables framework, a variety of methods and toolkits are available for impact evaluation. One particularly intuitive approach is matching, which has been discussed in various studies such as Rosenbaum and Rubin (1983, 1985), Heckman et al. (1998a,b), Dehejia and Wahba (1999), and Lechner et al. (2011). The basic idea behind matching is to identify and pair up observations that are similar (or, ideally, identical) in terms of their covariate values but differ in whether or not they received the intervention. This process creates a matched sample of treatment and control groups that are comparable in terms of their covariate values, just as it would in a randomized experiment. For example, for each individual in the treatment group participating in an employee training program, we aim to find a control group individual with similar covariate values X (e.g., age or education) to form a matched pair. By pairing up individuals in this way, we create treatment

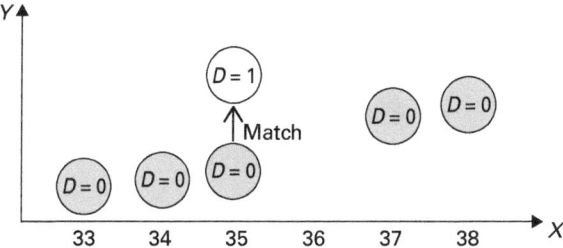

Figure 4.4
Pair matching based on age

and control groups that are similar in terms of observed characteristics. We can then compare the average outcomes, such as productivity, across the matched groups to evaluate the impact of the intervention. Applying pair matching to all employees in the sample yields the average treatment effect (ATE), as shown in equation (2.2) in chapter 2. However, if we apply pair matching to only the trained employees, we obtain the average treatment effect on the treated (ATET), as shown in equation (2.3).

Looking at figure 4.4, we can see a visual representation of how pair matching works. Imagine we want to find the best match for an employee who received the training intervention ($D = 1$) among employees who did not receive the training ($D = 0$), with the goal of finding the most similar match in terms of age, which we will assume for simplicity is the only observed covariate X. We can then take the average difference in performance outcomes between the trained employees and their matched, untrained counterparts to estimate the ATET—in other words, the average effect of the training intervention among those who actually received it. Of course, in reality, we want to find matches that are comparable across multiple covariates, such as age, education, and work experience. To accomplish this, we use specific metrics like the so-called Mahalanobis distance, which allows us to assess how similar or different two potential matches are across multiple characteristics, in order to find matches that closely resemble the treatment group in all relevant aspects. This process is depicted in figure 4.5, where figures in the treatment and control groups sharing the same color and size possess comparable values across multiple covariates and are matched, as indicated by the connecting lines.

In addition to pair matching, there are several other matching methods with their own strengths and weaknesses. One such approach is one-to-many or $1{:}M$ matching, where for each reference observation—for example, a subject receiving the intervention, we find multiple (rather than just one) matches in the control group that are similar in terms of covariates X. Figure 4.6 illustrates this approach for a single covariate X (like age) when $M = 2$—that is, when the two closest observations in the control group are matched to a reference observation receiving the intervention. Also in this case, we compare the average outcomes of the matched treatment and control groups to assess the causal effect of the intervention.

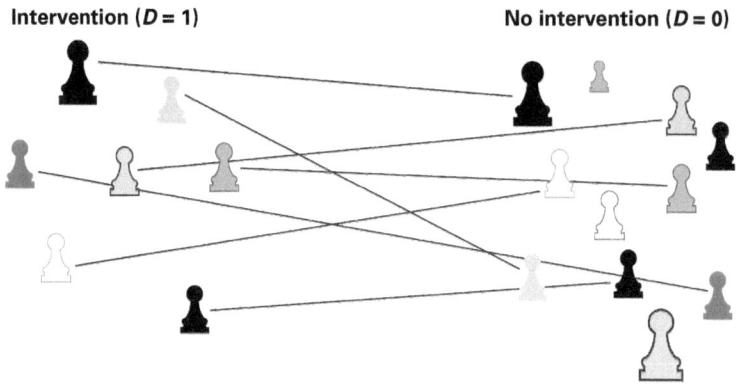

Figure 4.5
Pair matching

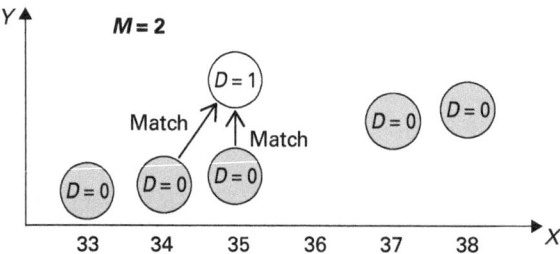

Figure 4.6
1:*M* matching

Another option is radius or caliper matching, which uses a minimum level of similarity rather than the number of closest matches as the matching criterion. For example, for a reference observation that is 36 years old, we might require that only observations within 1 year (i.e., between 35 to 37 years) be considered as matches. This method allows several observations to be used as matches, as long as they meet the similarity criterion for age (or other covariates).

The matching approaches discussed so far have a potential caveat: they require finding matches that are similar in all characteristics X, which can be challenging in practice when there are many characteristics to consider. For this reason, pair and 1:*M* matching may imply nonnegligible errors or biases when evaluating impacts even in large samples if X contains multiple continuous characteristics that take many distinct values, like income or wealth. This issue can be mitigated by combining matching with regression, which may correct certain biases (see Rubin, 1979 and Abadie and Imbens, 2011). As another alternative, Rosenbaum and Rubin (1983) propose propensity score matching for impact evaluation.

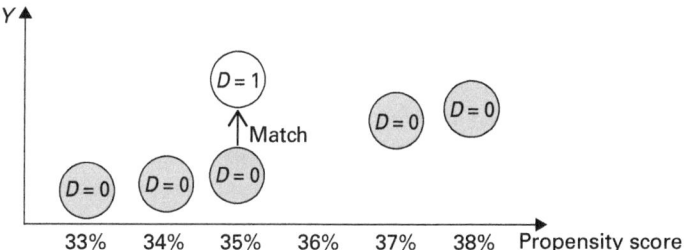

Figure 4.7
Propensity score matching

Rather than focusing on matching individuals based on their similarity in characteristics X, this approach involves matching observations based on their likelihood or probability of receiving the intervention, given their characteristics. This probability score is formally denoted by $\Pr(D=1|X)$, where Pr represents probability. In impact evaluation, $\Pr(D=1|X)$ is commonly known as a propensity score, thus resulting in the name propensity score matching. By adopting this approach, we can avoid the potential difficulties of finding matches that are similar in all characteristics and instead focus on finding matches that have a similar probability of receiving the intervention.

For instance, an employee who is 35 years old and has 12 years of education may have a similar probability of, say, 35% to participate in the training as an employee who is 25 years old and has 16 years of education. As their probabilities are similar, we may match these two individuals despite the age and education differences. In other words, we use the propensity score $\Pr(D=1|X)$, which takes values between 0 and 1 (or 0% and 100%, as it is a probability), as covariate to match employees in the treatment and control groups. In comparison to other matching approaches, propensity score matching has the advantage that the propensity score is just a single covariate, rather than a possibly large set of the employees' background characteristics. However, a disadvantage is that we need to measure any individual's propensity score in the data, which requires statistical modeling assumptions that may not perfectly capture human behavior. Estimating propensity scores typically involves regression methods such as probit or logit regression. Figure 4.7 illustrates how propensity score matching works, by considering a reference observation receiving the intervention with a propensity score of 35%. Then, we match this observation with the one in the control group that is most similar in terms of propensity score.

Matching estimators are not the only methods available for impact evaluation that aim to make the treatment and control groups comparable in terms of observed characteristics. We may also use regression as introduced in chapter 3, section 3.2, if we include the covariates X in the regression model. However, regression models can differ in their flexibility and the restrictions they impose on human behavior, depending on how covariates are accounted for. For instance, one restriction commonly imposed when using a linear regression is that the effect of a covariate on outcome Y is always the same, no matter how large X is. This implies, for instance, that a one-year change in age always induces the same change in the performance outcome, regardless of an employee's initial age. This assumption can be overly restrictive since an additional year may have different implications for younger and older individuals (e.g., 20- and 60-year-old employees). More flexible, so-called nonparametric regression techniques do not impose such assumptions but may require larger datasets than the more restrictive methods. Ultimately, the choice of regression model depends on the research question and the available data.

Formally, regression aims at estimating the ATE based on the following expression, which corresponds to the average of the difference of two regression models:

$$\Delta = E[E[Y|D=1,X] - E[Y|D=0,X]]. \quad (4.3)$$

In this equation, $E[Y|D=1,X]$ represents the average outcome (e.g., productivity) among individuals who received the intervention ($D=1$) and have specific characteristics X (such as age or education), as estimated by a regression model. Similarly, $E[Y|D=0,X]$ represents the average outcome among individuals who did not receive the intervention ($D=0$) and have specific characteristics X, also estimated by a regression model. Analogously, we obtain the ATET by averaging the difference in the regression models of individuals who received the intervention, where $D=1$:

$$\Delta_{D=1} = E\left[E[Y|D=1,X] - E[Y|D=0,X]|D=1\right] \quad (4.4)$$

$$= E\left[Y|D=1\right] - E[E[Y|D=0,X]|D=1].$$

The second equality in equation (4.4) is derived from a statistical law called iterated expectations. It shows that when measuring the ATET, it is sufficient to use a regression model for $E[Y|D=0,X]$, the outcome without intervention ($D=0$), whereas a model for $E[Y|D=1,X]$ is not necessarily required.

Weighting observations based on their propensity score is another approach for impact evaluation, which can be thought of as giving more importance to some observations than others depending on their likelihood of receiving the intervention. The goal is to gauge the importance or weights of observations with and without intervention such that after weighting, the treatment and control groups are similar in terms of their characteristics X. For calculating the ATE, this is achieved by scaling outcomes in the treatment and control groups by the inverse of (i.e., by one over) the propensity score to receive or not receive the intervention, respectively. This implies that observations with propensity scores that are under- or over represented in their respective group relative to the entire population are upgraded or downgraded, respectively, in terms of their weight (or importance). After the weighting step, we may simply compare the rescaled or reweighted outcomes in the treatment and control groups to measure the ATE. Because we use the inverse of the propensity score to reweigh observations, the method is called inverse probability weighting (IPW) and was originally proposed by Horvitz and Thompson (1952).

Selection on Observables: Aim to Compare Apples with Apples 47

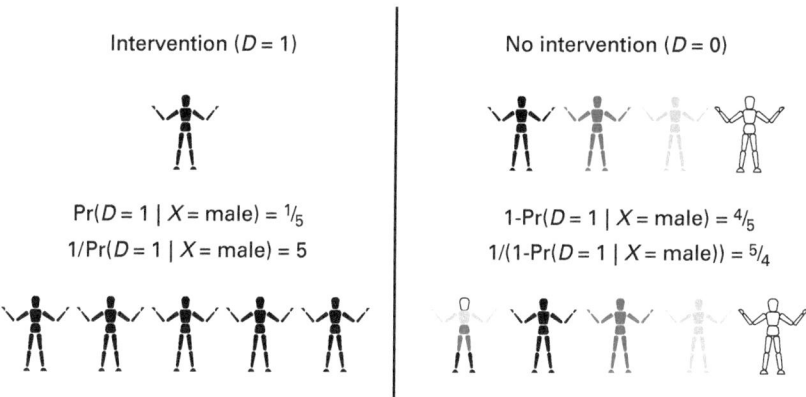

Figure 4.8
Inverse probability weighting

The methodology is depicted in figure 4.8, where we consider the propensity score $\Pr(D=1|X=male)$, representing the likelihood of receiving the intervention if the covariate gender (X) is equal to being male. Considering that there are five males in total, with one receiving the intervention, the probability of receiving the intervention when being male is $1/5$, formally denoted as $\Pr(D=1|X=male)=1/5$. Weighting the male receiving the intervention by the inverse of the propensity score results in $1/\Pr(D=1|X=male)=1/(1/5)=5$. Consequently, the single male is replicated five times to correspond to the overall number of males. Furthermore, among the five males in total, four do not receive the intervention. Therefore, the probability of not receiving the intervention when being male is $1-\Pr(D=1|X=male)=4/5$. Weighting each of those males by the inverse of this probability yields $1/(1-\Pr(D=1|X=male))=1/(4/5)=5/4$. Consequently, the four males without intervention are weighted by $5/4$, resulting in $5/4 \times 4 = 5$ males after reweighting. After this process, the number of males in the treatment and control groups is equal (to five), ensuring comparability of the groups with respect to the covariate X.

Formally, IPW identifies the ATE in the population based on the following equation:

$$\Delta = E\left[\frac{Y \cdot D}{\Pr(D=1|X)} - \frac{Y \cdot (1-D)}{1-\Pr(D=1|X)}\right]. \tag{4.5}$$

We may also apply IPW for measuring the ATET, based on the following expression:

$$\Delta_{D=1} = E\left[\frac{Y \cdot D}{\Pr(D=1)} - \frac{Y \cdot (1-D) \cdot \Pr(D=1|X)}{(1-\Pr(D=1|X)) \cdot \Pr(D=1)}\right], \tag{4.6}$$

where $\Pr(D=1)$ is the probability of receiving the intervention (or share of receivers) in the entire population.

Compared to matching, IPW has the advantage of being computationally fast—that is, i does not take much computer time even in large datasets. Additionally, IPW removes the need to make decisions about certain options such as the number of matches in one-to-many matching or the radius size in radius matching. However, there are some downsides to IPW. It can be unstable and prone to substantial errors in effect measurement if there are (many) observations in the dataset that have extreme propensity scores very close to one or zero (see for instance Khan and Tamer, 2010). This can, for example, occur if a significant portion of employees has almost no chance of participating in an intervention, such as training, due to their characteristics (e.g., education), leading to extremely low propensity scores. This implies that for those individuals with extremely low propensity scores, there are hardly any comparison observations who receive the intervention and have similar characteristics (like education).

In such cases, extreme propensity scores can throw a wrench into our data analysis, forcing us to get creative with our methods. One approach is to simply drop subjects with propensity scores that are too extreme and only keep those subjects whose characteristics X are such that there is a decent number of both intervention-receiving and nonreceiving observations. For example, we could trim the data by discarding individuals with propensity scores lower than 1% or higher than 99%, leaving only observations with scores between 1% and 99%. This trimming technique typically stabilizes the IPW method and reduces the likelihood of large errors caused by method variability. It is also useful for other approaches like matching and regression, even though they are generally less sensitive to extreme propensity scores. However, dropping subjects with extreme propensity scores also has its drawbacks: it means we can only conduct our impact evaluation on a subset of the initial sample. In other words, the impact we obtain may not be fully representative of the overall population.

It is even possible to combine several of the previously mentioned methods into a single research design. One increasingly popular impact evaluation approach is doubly robust (DR) estimation, which combines regression and weighting (IPW) (see, for instance, Robins et al., 1994, 1995, and Robins and Rotnitzky, 1995). This method simultaneously uses (i) a regression for modeling how the outcome is affected by the intervention and the covariates and (ii) IPW—that is, weighting observations based on their propensity score to receive the intervention. The method is aptly named "doubly robust" because it can accurately measure the impact of the intervention if either the regression model for the outcome or the propensity scores are correctly measured. In other words, it gives us two shots at getting a proper evaluation. If we get the outcome model right, then it does not matter if we make mistakes in estimating the propensity scores (at least if we have a large enough dataset). Alternatively, if we get the propensity scores right, then it does not matter if we get the outcome model wrong. Furthermore, DR estimation can even handle minor errors in both the outcome model and the propensity scores, as long as those errors are not too large. Mathematically speaking, this is because the mistakes in the two models enter the DR estimation in a multiplicative way, meaning that their product approaches zero if both errors are small.

More formally, the doubly robust (DR) estimation method evaluates the ATE (Δ) and the ATET ($\Delta_{D=1}$) using the following expressions:

Selection on Observables: Aim to Compare Apples with Apples

$$\Delta =$$
$$E\left[E[Y|D=1,X] - E[Y|D=0,X] + \frac{(Y-E[Y|D=1,X])\cdot D}{\Pr(D=1|X)} - \frac{(Y-E[Y|D=0,X])\cdot(1-D)}{1-\Pr(D=1|X)}\right],$$
$$\Delta_{D=1} = E\left[\frac{(Y-E[Y|D=0,X])\cdot D}{\Pr(D=1)} - \frac{(Y-E[Y|D=0,X])\cdot(1-D)\cdot\Pr(D=1|X)}{(1-\Pr(D=1|X))\cdot\Pr(D=1)}\right]. \qquad (4.7)$$

Here, $E[Y|D=1,X]$ refers to the average outcome (e.g., productivity) among individuals who received the intervention ($D=1$) and possess specific characteristics X (e.g., age or education), which is measured using a regression model. Similarly, $E[Y|D=0,X]$ denotes the average outcome among individuals who did not receive the intervention ($D=0$) and have particular characteristics X. The previously discussed propensity score, $\Pr(D=1|X)$, is the probability of receiving the intervention. As discussed before, the DR method can be expected to perform well in large enough datasets if we either the outcome regression models ($E[Y|D=1,X]$ and $E[Y|D=0,X]$) or the propensity scores ($\Pr(D=1|X)$) right. It can also work well even when there are limited errors in modeling all of $E[Y|D=1,X]$, $E[Y|D=0,X]$, and $\Pr(D=1|X)$, a property known as Neyman (1959) orthogonality.

The previously discussed methods can also be useful if there is not only one intervention to be evaluated (i.e., comparing outcomes with and without intervention), but if we are dealing with multiple interventions, like different employee training programs. For instance, we may use the previously described matching, weighting, or DR approaches to perform pairwise comparisons of any intervention (e.g., an IT training, a sales training, a project management course, and so on) with no intervention. Furthermore, we can also apply appropriately adjusted versions of the methods for assessing different magnitudes or intensities of some intervention even if it can take (even infinitely) many different values, such as the impact of 20, 30, or 40 hours of IT training on productivity. For example, a regression model can be used to assess how average productivity changes when providing 20 or 30 hours of training versus no training, while also making individuals with different levels of training comparable in their observed characteristics X, in order to properly assess the effect of the intervention. Alternatively, IPW or DR methods can also be used to evaluate such interventions with (infinitely) many values (i.e., interventions that are, statistically speaking, continuously distributed), as discussed in Flores et al. (2012) and Kennedy et al. (2017). However, from a practical standpoint, employing such methods necessitates a sufficiently large dataset with a diverse range of intervention values to yield a satisfactory performance of impact evaluation.

4.4 Use Cases in R

We subsequently apply the previously discussed methods to evaluate the impact of a marketing intervention—namely, a retailer's coupon campaigns—on customers' daily purchases.

To this end, we analyze a subset of the retailer's sales previously considered in Langen and Huber (2023) that originally come from the AmExpert 2019 Machine Learning Hackathon AML (2019). The database contains information about how many coupons a customer received in a specific coupon campaign, the customer's daily expenditures in the period related to the campaign, and additional customer characteristics such as past purchases, income, age, and family size. Our intervention is defined as receiving at least one coupon during a campaign versus not receiving any coupon. We first consider impact evaluation based on regression. To this end, we load several previously installed packages using the *library* command: *causalweight*, *lmtest*, and *sandwich*.

We analyze the *coupon* dataset from the *causalweight* package, which we load using the command *data(coupon)*. The dataset consists of 1,293 observations and 9 variables—that is, the expenditure outcome (*dailyspending*), the intervention (*coupons*), which equals 1 if a customer received any coupons and 0 if this is not the case, and 7 more customer characteristics that serve as covariates. We estimate a linear regression model of daily spending on all covariates in the dataset with the command *lm(formula=dailyspending ~ ., data=coupon)*. The dot after "~" implies that the outcome *dailyspending* is modeled as a function of all remaining variables in the dataset. Furthermore, the argument *data=coupon* specifies the dataset in which the outcome, intervention, and characteristics can be found. The regression results are stored in an R object named *results*. Finally, we run the *coeftest* command from the *lmtest* package with the argument *vcov = vcovHC* to display the impact and its *p*-value. The code below provides the R code for each of the steps:

```
library(causalweight)                              # load causalweight package
library(lmtest)                                    # load lmtest package
library(sandwich)                                  # load sandwich package
data(coupon)                                       # load coupon data
results=lm(formula=dailyspending~., data=coupon)   # run linear regression
coeftest(results, vcov=vcovHC)                     # show impact
```

Running the R code yields the following output:

	Estimate	Std. Error	t value	Pr(>|t|)	
(Intercept)	170.76054	40.69064	4.1966	2.896e−05	***
coupons	73.64120	23.39623	3.1476	0.001684	**
coupons_preperiod	−22.65124	24.74873	−0.9152	0.360233	

```
dailyspending_preperiod    0.12004   0.02967   4.0459  5.522e-05 ***
income_bracket            19.62303   4.25100   4.6161  4.302e-06 ***
age_range                -16.08268   6.05696  -2.6552  0.008023  **
married                   40.04585  19.56255   2.0471  0.040855  *
rented                    11.37793  28.19776   0.4035  0.686644
family_size                1.40647   9.26952   0.1517  0.879423
---
Signif. codes:  0 '***' 0.001 '**' 0.01 '*' 0.05 '.' 0.1 ' ' 1
```

The estimated impact of receiving coupons versus not receiving any coupons is shown in the first column of the *coupons* row and is roughly 73.64. This implies that, on average, customers spend an additional $73.64 per day if they receive a coupon (assuming daily spending is measured in dollars, but it may be a different currency). The corresponding *p*-value provided in the last column is 0.001684. This indicates that in light of the estimated impact obtained from our database, the chance of the true impact being zero for the entire customer population is very low. This strong evidence for a nonzero, positive effect of coupons on customer spending is highlighted by the two stars (**) at the end of the row, indicating statistical significance at the 1% significance level. Thus, the error probability of incorrectly claiming a nonzero effect in the population does not exceed 1%.

Next, we use pair matching to analyze the impact of coupons on sales. To do this, we install and load the *Matching* package using the *install.packages* and *library* commands. We then define the outcome, treatment, and covariates as their own R objects to be used in the matching procedure. To accomplish this, we create an outcome variable named *y*, which corresponds to the first column in the *coupon* dataset, containing the customers' daily expenditures (the variable *dailyspending*). We run the command *y=coupon[,1]* to do this. Regarding the use of the square brackets, *[,1]*, the first argument (before the comma) selects a specific row or observation in our data, while the second argument (after the comma) selects a specific column or variable of the *coupon* data. The first argument is not defined (i.e., it is left blank) so that we select all observations, while the second argument is set to 1 so that we select the first variable (for all observations), which is *dailyspending*. We also define an intervention variable named *d*, which corresponds to the second column (or variable) in our *coupon* data named *coupons* (which is 1 for customers receiving coupons and 0 for those not receiving any coupons): *d=coupon[,2]*. Furthermore, we define the covariates (named *x*) as a data matrix of variables that correspond to variables 3 to 9 in the *coupon* data: *x=as.matrix(coupon[,3:9])*. The *as.matrix* command is used to define a matrix of numeric variables. Note that we may run all these variable definitions in just one line if we separate them by a semicolon (;).

We then run the *Match* command for pair matching, whose first argument, named *Y*, corresponds to the outcome, which we set to our outcome variable *y*: *Y=y*. The second argument in the *Match* command (separated from the first one by a comma) is named *Tr* and corresponds to the intervention (or treatment), so we set it to our treatment variable: *Tr=d*. The third argument, *X*, corresponds to the covariates, which we set to our covariates *x*: *X=x*. The fourth (and last) argument that we specify is *estimand*, the kind of impact that we want to estimate. As we are interested in the ATE (i.e., the average impact), we set *estimand="ATE"*. Finally, we save the results in an R object named *results* and wrap the latter with the *summary* command to display the estimated impact. The box below provides the R code for each of the steps.

```
install.packages("Matching")                                    # install package
library(Matching)                                               # load Matching package
y=coupon[,1]; d=coupon[,2]; x=as.matrix(coupon[,3:9])           # define variables
results=Match(Y=y, Tr=d,X=x, estimand="ATE")                    # pair matching
summary(results)                                                # show impact
```

Running the R code yields the following output.

```
Estimate...  60.074
AI SE......  27.707
T-stat.....  2.1682
p.val......  0.030147
```

The first line of the results provides the estimate of the ATE (see *Estimate*), which amounts to approximately $60.07. The fourth line shows the *p*-value (*p.val*), which equals 0.03. Therefore, the likelihood of the true effect being zero is below 5% based on our estimate. Like for our previously considered regression approach, matching provides us with strong statistical evidence supporting a positive impact of coupons on daily customer expenditure.

Next, we will estimate the ATE using IPW as outlined in equation (4.5) with the *treatweight* command from the *causalweight* package. Similar to the *Match* command, the first, second, and third arguments of the *treatweight* command are the outcome (*y*), treatment (*d*), and covariates (*x*), respectively. We store the estimation output in an R object named *results*. The code for each step is provided in the box below.

Selection on Observables: Aim to Compare Apples with Apples

```
results=treatweight(y=y, d=d, x=x)            # run IPW
```

Once the code has been run, we can access any output generated by the *treatweight* command and stored in *results* by using the *$* sign. For example, *results$effect* contains the ATE estimate, and *results$pval* contains the *p*-value. The following R code shows how to access these objects.

```
results$effect; results$pval                  # show impact and p-value
[1] 80.94421
[1] 0.001677651
```

The IPW estimation suggests that providing coupons boosts daily expenditure per customer by approximately $80.94. The *p*-value is almost zero (0.16%), such that we can reject the null hypothesis with very little chance of error. Note that the *p*-value may slightly vary with each application of the IPW procedure, as the computation of the *p*-value is based on a method called bootstrapping, which has some random component. Nonetheless, in each attempt, the *p*-value will be very low.

Finally, we run doubly robust (DR) estimation based on equation (4.7). To this end, we first install and load the *drgee* package. We then run the *drgee* command with two required arguments. The first argument, *oformula*, specifies a model for the outcome as a function of the covariates, excluding the intervention (even though the latter will be ultimately included in the estimation). We use the formula *oformula=formula(y~x)* for this purpose. The second argument, *eformula*, specifies a propensity score model for the intervention variable as a function of the covariates: *eformula=formula(d~x)*. We estimate this model using logistic regression, which is suitable for variables that take only the values 1 or 0 (i.e., binary variables), as is the case for our intervention *d*. To this end, we set the third argument, *elink*, to a logit regression: *elink="logit"*. We store the output of the *drgee* command in an R object named *results* and wrap it with the *summary* command to inspect the ATE estimate. The R code for each step is presented in the box below.

```
install.packages(c("drgee"))                                              # install packages
library(drgee)                                                            # load drgee package
results=drgee(oformula=formula(y~x), eformula=formula(d~x), elink="logit") # DR
summary(results)                                                          # show impact
```

Running the code yields the following output.

```
    Estimate  Std. Error  z value  Pr(>|z|)
d    74.84      23.31      3.211    0.00132 **
---
Signif. codes:  0 '***' 0.001 '**' 0.01 '*' 0.05 '.' 0.1 ' ' 1
```

The ATE estimate suggests that coupons increase average daily spending by $74.84, and in light of our estimate, the chance that the true impact in the population is actually zero is very low (with the *p*-value amounting to just 0.13%). While the estimates of the causal effect obtained from DR, IPW, matching, and regression are not identical, they all provide strong evidence of a positive impact of issuing coupons on customer spending.

4.5 Use Cases in Python

This section provides the Python implementation for the use cases discussed in the previous section, 4.4 (where we used R), which involves evaluating the impact of a marketing intervention, specifically coupon campaigns, on customers' daily purchases. We start by importing the *pandas* and *statsmodels* libraries and loading the *coupon.csv* dataset into a Pandas dataframe named *df* using the *read_csv* function. We define as variables X all variables in the dataset but *dailyspending*, which we exclude from X using the *command df.columns != 'dailyspending'*. Next, we add a constant term to X (for the linear regression to be conducted) using the command *sm.add_constant(X)*. We define the outcome variable Y to correspond to *dailyspending*.

We run a linear regression using the *OLS(Y, X).fit(cov_type = 'HC0')* command from the *statsmodels* library. The results are stored in a Python object named *results*, and we use the *print* command to display the regression output in *results.summary()*. The Python code for each step is presented in the box below. The estimated impact suggests that, on average, receiving a coupon increases sales per customer by $73.64 per day, which aligns with the results of the first use case in R from the previous section.

```python
import pandas as pd                                    # load pandas library
import statsmodels.api as sm                           # load statsmodels library
df = pd.read_csv('data/coupon.csv')                    # load coupon data
X = df.loc[:, df.columns != 'dailyspending']           # define regressors
```

Selection on Observables: Aim to Compare Apples with Apples

```
X = sm.add_constant(X)                          # add a constant
Y = df['dailyspending']                         # define outcome
results = sm.OLS(Y, X).fit(cov_type = 'HC0')    # run linear regression
print(results.summary())                        # show results
```

In a next step, we implement pair matching in Python to assess the ATE of coupon receipt on customer spending. Initially, we import *CausalModel* from the *causalinference* library, featuring a pair matching algorithm, as well as *pandas* and *numpy*. Upon loading the coupon data into a Pandas dataframe named *df*, the outcome variable Y is specified as *dailyspending*, and the intervention variable D is specified as *coupons*. The covariates X encompass all variables except *dailyspending* and *coupons*. In the subsequent step, we define the causal model, incorporating Y, D, and X using the *CausalModel* command and store it in a Python object named *model*.

We proceed by executing pair matching, setting the number of matches to one, through the *est_via_matching* function. Finally, we present the matching output using the command *print(model.estimates)*. The estimated ATE is approximately $60.07, equivalent to the impact observed in the second R-based use case in section 4.4, although the *p*-value is slightly higher. This discrepancy arises due to variations in the method used to estimate the matching estimator's variance or uncertainty, differing from the previous approach. The box below comprises the Python code for each step.

```
from causalinference import CausalModel                              # load causalmodel
import pandas as pd                                                  # load pandas library
import numpy as np                                                   # load numpy library
df = pd.read_csv('data/coupon.csv')                                  # load coupon data
Y = np.asarray(df['dailyspending'])                                  # select outcome
D = np.asarray(df['coupons'])                                        # select treatment
X = np.asarray(df.drop(['dailyspending', 'coupons'], axis=1))        # select covariates
model = CausalModel(Y,D,X)                                           # create causal model
model.est_via_matching(weights='inv', matches=1)                     # pair matching
print(model.estimates)                                               # matching output
```

Next, we estimate the ATE using inverse probability weighting (IPW). In addition to the *pandas* library for data manipulation, we load the *dowhy* library, which incorporates IPW for impact evaluation. After loading the coupon data into a Pandas dataframe named *df*, we define the covariates *X* by excluding the variables *dailyspending* and *coupons*. Next, we create a causal model using the *CausalModel* command in the *dowhy* library to specify the intervention (*treatment*), the outcome variable (*outcome*), and the covariates (*common_causes*) to be considered, saving it in a Python object named *model*. We then execute the *identify_effect* command to identify the causal effect to be estimated (the impact of the intervention on the outcome by controlling for the covariates) and store the output in an object named *identified_estimand*. The latter is utilized in the *estimate_effect* command to estimate the ATE, specifying *method_name = 'backdoor.propensity_score_weighting'* to run IPW.

We store the results in an object named *estimate* and use the commands *print(estimate.value)* and *print(estimate.test_stat_significance())* to display the estimated ATE and its *p*-value, respectively. The impact of receiving coupons on daily customer spending amounts to 76.43, which is relatively close to the results obtained from the R-based IPW estimation in the third use case of section 4.4. Furthermore, the *p*-value is close to zero (0.003), allowing us to safely reject a zero impact in the customer population from which our sample is drawn. The box below provides the Python code for each step.

```python
import pandas as pd                                          # load pandas library
import dowhy as dw                                           # load dowhy library
df = pd.read_csv('data/coupon.csv')                          # load coupon data
X = df.drop(['dailyspending', 'coupons'], axis = 1)          # select covariates
model = dw.CausalModel(data = df,                            # create model
    treatment = 'coupons',                                   # specify treatment
    outcome = 'dailyspending',                               # specify outcome
    common_causes = list(X.columns))                         # specify covariates
identified_estimand = model.identify_effect()                # identify the effect
estimate = model.estimate_effect(identified_estimand,        # IPW
    method_name = 'backdoor.propensity_score_weighting',
    target_units = 'ate',
    method_params = {'weighting_scheme': 'ips_weight'})
print(estimate.value)                                        # show impact
print(estimate.test_stat_significance())                     # show p-value
```

Finally, we implement doubly robust (DR) estimation using the *DoubleML* library, which we load in addition to the *pandas* and *sklearn* libraries. After reading the coupon data into a

Selection on Observables: Aim to Compare Apples with Apples

Pandas dataframe, we define the covariates (*X*) in the same way as in the previous examples. Next, we use the *DoubleMLData* command to generate a data object from the coupon data, specifying the outcome (*y_col*), intervention (*d_cols*), and covariates (*x_cols*) and save it as *dml_data*. Two statistical models are then defined: one for the outcome (*ml_l*, a linear regression model) and the other for the intervention (*ml_m*, a logistic regression model).

We feed the data and statistical models into the *DoubleMLPLR* procedure and run the *fit()* command to estimate the ATE, saving the output in an object named *dr*. Finally, we apply the *print* command to the *summary* attribute of the *dr* object to display the results. The ATE amounts to $74.11, with a very low *p*-value of just 0.0013, which is very close to the R-based results obtained in the last use case of section 4.4. The Python code for each step is given in the box below.

```python
import pandas as pd                              # load pandas library
import doubleml as dml                           # load doubleml library
from sklearn import linear_model                 # import models from sklearn
df = pd.read_csv('data/coupon.csv')              # load coupon data
X = df.drop(['dailyspending', 'coupons'], axis=1) # select covariates
dml_data = dml.DoubleMLData(df,                  # create object from coupon data
y_col = 'dailyspending',                         # define outcome
d_cols = 'coupons',                              # define intervention
x_cols = list(X.columns.values))                 # define covariates
ml_l = linear_model.LinearRegression()           # define model for outcome
ml_m = linear_model.LogisticRegression()         # define model for intervention
dr = dml.DoubleMLPLR(dml_data,                   # DR estimation
ml_l,
ml_m).fit()
print(dr.summary)                                # show the results
```

5 Causal Machine Learning

5.1 Motivating Causal Machine Learning

In chapter 4, we discussed various methods for impact evaluation, which involve creating treatment and control groups that are comparable with respect to observed characteristics, represented by X. To do this, analysts or researchers must determine which characteristics to use in order to make the two groups comparable (e.g., age or education) in advance—that is, prior to the analysis. This requires a deep understanding of the domain to identify which characteristics satisfy the selection-on-observables assumption, meaning that these covariates reflect all factors that are associated with both the intervention and the outcome. Often, these characteristics are selected based on intuition, theoretical reasoning, or previous analyses.

For example, consider a company aiming to evaluate the impact of offering discounts on sales. In this scenario, the company may observe characteristics like customer demographics (such as age and location, among others) and purchase history (previous purchases and product preferences) in a customer database. It could be assumed that only these observed characteristics (but no unobserved factors) jointly influence discount receipt (treatment) and the sales per customer (outcome), which may appear plausible if the company possesses information about which characteristics actually affect the likelihood of receiving a discount. For instance, based on internal rules, customers within certain geographical regions or with particular purchase histories might have a higher likelihood of receiving a discount. Such domain-specific knowledge aids in selecting characteristics that are relevant for forming comparable treatment and control groups (by controlling for these observed characteristics that influence discount receipt).

In many, if not most, impact evaluations, however, it may be far from clear which set of characteristics is sufficient (if such a set exists at all) to satisfy the selection-on-observables assumption, which requires that the intervention is as good as random after making groups comparable in these characteristics. This is particularly true in big data contexts where a large number of characteristics are collected. With the rise of digitization, this is becoming more common in many evaluation contexts, such as scanner data in supermarkets and online tracking of customer behavior. While a wealth of consumer characteristics can be generated by such technologies, not all of them may be equally important in the context of impact evaluation. In fact, a subset of characteristics that is unknown beforehand might be sufficient to satisfy the selection-on-observables assumption. As a result, a method that can learn from the data which subset of characteristics should be considered to make treated and control groups comparable is attractive, provided that the available characteristics are informative enough to allow such a set to exist.

A further and related issue is that because analysts typically do not have a perfect idea about which characteristics to include, they tend to select them according to ad hoc rules related to how strongly the characteristics are associated with the intervention and/or the outcome. For example, an analyst may investigate whether characteristics like age or education are important for access to a marketing intervention, such as a loyalty card, or for an outcome like purchasing behavior. Analysts typically consider different sets of characteristics and choose the one that appears optimal based on their ad hoc rule. Unfortunately, impact evaluation based on the previously discussed methods is generally not robust to "snooping" across characteristics to satisfy ad hoc rules. This implies that conclusions about the size and existence of a causal effect may be unreliable when using ad hoc rules made by the analyst, as these methods rely on the (mostly unrealistic) assumption that the analyst knows the characteristics in advance, rather than snooping across them. In statistical terms, the estimated effects and their associated uncertainty (i.e., variance) may be biased due to the analyst's preselection of characteristics, which is commonly referred to as the pre-testing problem. It is therefore desirable to have a method that can learn the set of characteristics in a way that avoids compromising the causal conclusions, in contrast to using ad hoc rules.

An exciting subfield of artificial intelligence named causal machine learning (which is to be distinguished from conventional predictive machine learning) can avoid the previously mentioned issues, given that certain conditions are met. Causal machine learning (CML) selects important characteristics from a potentially vast pool of variables in a data-driven way to make the treatment and control groups comparable in these selected characteristics. However, it must be emphasized that CML is not a magic bullet that can do away with the fundamental requirements of impact evaluation. Like for the methods outlined in chapter 4, the information in the data must be sufficiently rich to satisfy the selection-on-observables assumption in expression (4.1). For instance, this assumption would fail if certain unobserved personality traits of customers (e.g., impulsivity) influenced the receipt of discounts (treatment) as well as subsequent purchasing behavior (outcome). In such a scenario, establishing comparable treatment and control groups based solely on observed characteristics would generally be impossible.

However, if the selection-on-observables assumption does indeed hold, then we may fruitfully apply CML if we do not know in advance which of the (possibly many) observed characteristics are the crucial ones for making treatment and control groups comparable. In other words, CML can learn the subset of characteristics that are most relevant for ensuring comparability between the treatment and control groups, without requiring prior knowledge about which characteristics to include. Under the condition that a, relative to the size of the data, not too large number of characteristics can account for the most important factors affecting the intervention and outcome, CML can be highly competitive. Being competitive means that, despite the challenging task of learning important characteristics from the data, CML can estimate the average impact (ATE) as well as a method that relies on knowing the appropriate set of characteristics to be included (or controlled for) a priori, without any data-driven learning. In other words, CML does not compromise the performance compared to knowing the crucial characteristics beforehand if those characteristics are not excessively numerous relative to the number of subjects in the data.

This is particularly advantageous when we lack prior knowledge of all crucial characteristics for ensuring comparability between the treatment and control groups. For example, in scenarios where numerous customer demographics are observed, but it is uncertain which ones importantly influence both the intervention (e.g., receiving a discount) and the outcome (e.g., sales), CML can be used under the assumption that the important characteristics are available within the dataset. Huber et al. (2022), for instance, apply CML to evaluate the impact of train discounts in Switzerland on demand shifts, measured as rescheduling of train trips to a different time than initially planned. They observe many demand-related factors in the data that may affect both the discount intervention and the demand shift outcome, including train class, month, weekday, time of day, public holidays, distance, and trip-specific points of departure and arrival. Each combination of departure and arrival could be considered as a separate characteristic, entailing a large number of variables that could be potentially used to make treatment and control groups comparable. This motivates the use of CML to account for characteristics importantly affecting the intervention or the outcome in a data-driven manner.

In addition to measuring average impacts in a population such as employees or customers, CML can also be used to analyze how impacts differ across different subpopulations. This is known as moderation or heterogeneity analysis, as we aim to discover whether, for example, a marketing campaign is more effective for one customer segment than another, where customer segments are defined in terms of observed characteristics X (such as age, previous purchasing history, and so on). For example, consider a marketing campaign that offers discounts on a product or service. CML can be used to uncover whether this campaign has a differential impact on different customer segments, based on observed characteristics like age or previous purchase history. It might turn out that the discount is more effective in boosting sales among customers who have previously purchased less, compared to customers who have been faithful and made many high-value purchases. This kind of heterogeneity analysis can help to better target different customer segments and improve the overall effectiveness of the campaign.

Langen and Huber (2023) apply CML to evaluate the impact of coupons issued by a retailer on purchases per customer and analyze effect heterogeneity across different customer

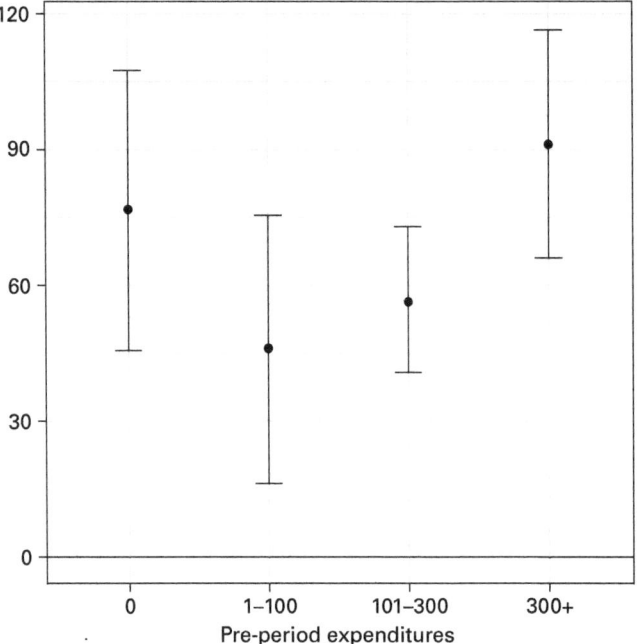

Figure 5.1
Effect heterogeneity across past purchases

segments. Specifically, they investigate how the average impact of the coupon intervention depends on customers' age, income, family size, and precampaign expenditures. One finding is that the impact is more pronounced among customers who made either no or rather large purchases in the period prior to the campaign. This is illustrated in figure 5.1, which depicts the average impacts across different customer groups defined in terms of past purchases, with dots representing the impact estimates and bands representing the 95% confidence intervals.

Finally, CML enables us to go beyond just identifying varying responses to marketing interventions across customer segments. Under certain conditions, CML also allows us to optimize the targeting strategy across customer segments in terms of which segments should or should not receive the intervention, such as discounts, possibly also taking costs into account. By learning the optimal policy that balances the impact and the costs of the intervention, we can maximize the net benefits of the marketing campaign. This means that companies can learn to more efficiently allocate their resources and achieve better results with their marketing efforts. For instance, Langen and Huber (2023) apply an optimal policy learning algorithm to detect customer groups that should be targeted optimally by coupon campaigns in such a way that the overall purchases by customers are maximized. Based on data-driven customer segmentation, the results suggest that the optimal targeting strategy varies across customer characteristics like income, preintervention expenditures, and family size.

5.2 Elements of Causal Machine Learning

The term causal machine learning (CML) is derived from the fact that the statistical models for the intervention and the outcome are obtained from machine learning techniques. Specifically, this concerns models for the propensity score $\Pr(D=1|X)$, which is the likelihood of receiving the intervention given the observed characteristics, as well as the conditional mean outcomes $E[Y|D=1,X]$ and $E[Y|D=0,X]$, which represent the average outcome (e.g., purchasing behavior) among subjects with a specific set of characteristics X (e.g., 30 years of education) and a specific value of the intervention (e.g., $D=1$ for receiving a discount). As previously mentioned, machine learning can learn the important characteristics in X that have a large influence on both receiving the intervention and the outcome from the data.

Once we have obtained the machine learning-based models for $\Pr(D=1|X)$, $E[Y|D=1,X]$, and $E[Y|D=0,X]$, we can use them to estimate the average impact of the intervention, such as on all customers or only those who received the marketing intervention. This estimation can be achieved using the doubly robust (DR) expressions (equation (4.7)) discussed in section 4.3 in chapter 4. As discussed in Chernozhukov et al. (2018), this approach is known as double machine learning (DML) and can perform as well as if the analyst already knew the important characteristics in X a priori, provided certain conditions are met. These conditions include having a limited number of important characteristics compared to the number of subjects in the data, as it can be difficult for machine learning to identify all the important characteristics if there are too many of them in relation to the size of the data.

The reason why DML (like other CML approaches) can perform so well is because by using DR expressions for impact evaluation, one can allow for a limited amount of errors when setting up statistical models for the intervention and the outcomes as discussed in section 4.3 in chapter 4. Even if machine learning does not work perfectly and might miss some characteristics influencing the marketing intervention or the purchasing outcome, the combination of both models (for the intervention and the outcome) can still yield a well-performing method for impact evaluation under certain conditions. Statistically speaking, this is because the errors in the models for the intervention and the outcome enter the DR method multiplicatively, so if errors in both models are relatively small, their product is close to zero. Intuitively, this implies that CML might ignore some less influential characteristics (whose influence is nevertheless not zero) but still yield a very decent impact evaluation, if it succeeds in detecting the (presumably not too numerous) set of very influential characteristics. In contrast, other methods, like matching, IPW, or regression, can be very sensitive to even small errors in the treatment or outcome models. For this reason, CML typically uses DR expressions like those in equation (4.7) or related DR approaches, rather than standard matching, IPW, or regression methods, which may perform poorly when combined with machine learning.

Another element of several CML approaches, including DML, is the idea of performing different tasks in different parts of the data. For example, we may randomly divide our dataset (which consists of, say, 4,000 customers) into two subsamples of 2,000 customers each. In the first subsample, we use machine learning to learn the statistical models for the intervention and the outcome. In the second subsample, we evaluate the impact of the intervention by integrating the learned models (from the first subsample) into the DR approach based on equation (4.7). We may then swap the tasks performed in the two subsamples in a second step to measure the impact in the first subsample, too. Finally, we take the average of the impact over both subsamples. For example, if the impact is $490 in the first subsample and $510 in the second subsample, then the average impact in the entire dataset is $500.

But why should we split our dataset into two subsamples? It may seem like a strange exercise at first glance, but there is a good reason behind it that is important for a decent performance of CML. By splitting the dataset into two subsamples, we can avoid a pitfall in statistical analysis called overfitting. Overfitting occurs when different steps in the analysis process, such as finding the important characteristics and measuring the impact of the intervention, are applied to the same dataset. This creates a statistical association (more specifically, a correlation) between the different steps, which can increase the variability or decrease the stability of impact evaluation across different datasets. It turns out that we can mitigate this issue by running the two different tasks of detecting important characteristics and measuring the impact of the intervention in the two different subsamples, then swapping the tasks in the data, and finally, taking the average of the impacts measured in both subsamples, a procedure known as cross-fitting. Figure 5.2 provides a graphical illustration of the cross-fitting workflow.

5.3 A Brief Introduction to Several Machine Learning Algorithms

Up to this point, we have not discussed what the machine learning algorithms look like that could be used for our purpose—that is, as an ingredient for estimating the intervention and outcome models in a CML procedure. In fact, numerous machine learning techniques are available that could be employed to identify the important covariates that influence the intervention or outcome. Here, we will briefly explain some of these techniques. One of the most intuitive approaches is using decision trees, as discussed in Morgan and Sonquist (1963) and Breiman et al. (1984). Decision trees work by recursively (i.e., repeatedly) splitting the dataset based on the values of characteristics X, such that the values of the intervention or outcome are as similar as possible within the newly created subsets.

For instance, if most of the older customers receive a discount while few of the young ones receive it, then the algorithm will split the data according to age. This means that within the created subsets, the subjects are similar in terms of the intervention value—meaning mostly

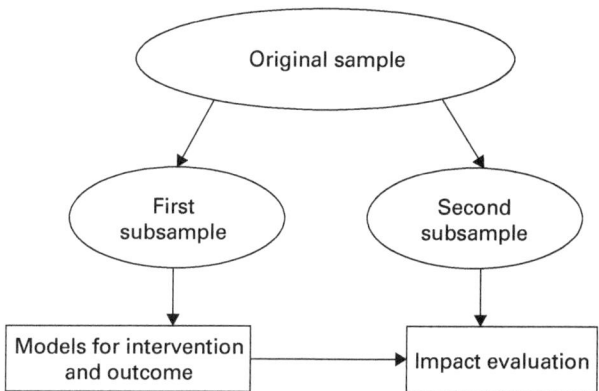

- In a second step, the roles of the subsamples are swapped: intervention/outcome models obtained in second subsample and impact evaluated in first subsample.
- In a third step, the impacts obtained in both subsamples are averaged.

Figure 5.2
Cross-fitting for impact evaluation

no discounts in the younger subset and predominantly discounts in the older subset. Splitting based on age indicates that age is an important characteristic, as it heavily influences receipt of the intervention. This recursive approach is then applied to divide the database into finer and finer subsets based on observed characteristics like age, education, gender, and so on. As a result, we obtain subsets that are more and more homogeneous based on the values of the intervention. The obtained splitting rules are then displayed as a decision tree, which gives the method its name.

The process of splitting the data can be repeated, creating or "growing" a decision tree that describes how the subsets are generated. A specific stopping rule, such as reaching a maximum number of subsets or a minimum number of subjects in a subset, can be used to terminate the process. However, the optimal number of subsets can also be determined in a data-driven way through a statistical method called validation. This involves dividing the dataset into two or more parts and carrying out different tasks on each part, such as growing the trees and evaluating their performance in modeling the marketing intervention. (This idea of performing different tasks in different parts is related to the idea of cross-fitting discussed at the end of section 5.2 and has the same goal of avoiding overfitting bias.) After the process of splitting to define subsets has finished, we can utilize the intervention values observed within a given subset to predict the intervention for subjects whose characteristics fall into that same subset. For instance, if we have a subset of younger, better-educated customers and most of them receive a discount, then our prediction or best guess is that

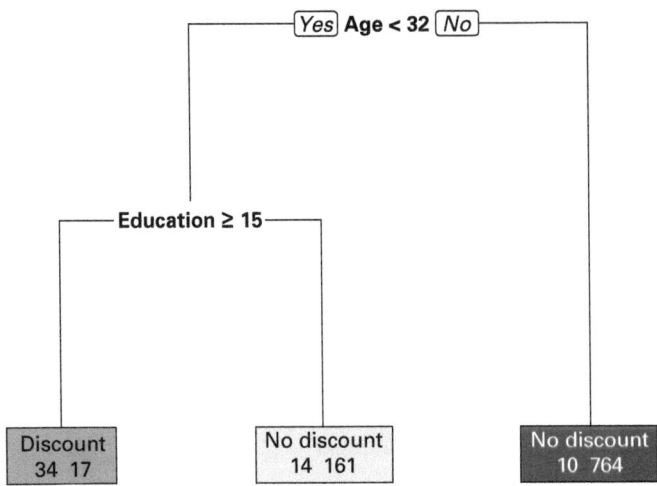

Figure 5.3
Decision tree

young and better-educated customers obtain a discount. We note that the subsets finally obtained from a tree are referred to as "leaves."

Figure 5.3 provides an example of a decision tree that predicts whether customers are likely to receive a discount or not based on their age and education level. The tree has two splits: the first split occurs at an age of 32 years, with customers younger than this age being more likely to receive a discount. Within the younger customers, the second split occurs at an education level of 15 years, with customers having less education being less likely to get a discount. Each resulting subset, or leaf, contains a prediction of whether the customers in that leaf are likely to obtain the discount or not. The subsets also contain the numbers of discount recipients (left number) and nonrecipients (right number). For instance, in the first subset (from the left) of customers who are younger than 32 and have at least 15 years of education, 34 customers do receive the discount, while 17 do not. The prediction is thus "discount" because the majority of customers get it.

Ideally, we want to validate how well prediction works among customers who are not included (in the data used for) the decision tree creation process but could potentially be of interest in the future, such as new potential customers. That is, we aim to have a method that can accurately predict the likelihood of receiving a discount for customers in other data than the first part of our sample, which we used for growing the decision tree. To achieve this, we use the second part of the data to compare the performance of different decision trees with varying numbers of splitting rules that we generated in the first part of the data. That is, we compare the predicted intervention (e.g., expected discount receipt among young and better-educated customers according to a tree) to the actual intervention values (e.g., observed discount receipt among young and better educated customers, in the second part of the data).

If the predicted values closely match the actual values, then the tree has high accuracy in terms of prediction. Conversely, if the predictions frequently do not correspond to the true intervention values, the accuracy of the tree is low. Ultimately, we choose the tree or splitting structure that yields the highest accuracy. Similar to cross-fitting, we can switch the roles of the two parts of the data. This implies that as a second validation step, we use the second part of the data to grow the trees and the first part to assess the accuracy of the predictions relative to the true intervention values. We can then average the accuracy from both parts of the data to find the best-performing tree, a technique known as cross-validation.

Decision trees, as we have just described them, are typically not among the most accurate machine learning methods out there. However, they can still be useful building blocks for more sophisticated models that make more accurate predictions about variables like interventions. Here's how it works: We randomly select a subsample of our original dataset (e.g., 2,000 out of 4,000 customers in our database) and use it to grow a decision tree to predict the intervention. We repeat this process of selecting a random subsample and growing a tree multiple times, say 1,000 times. We then combine the predictions of all 1,000 trees into a single aggregate or average prediction, which often has higher accuracy and provides a better statistical model for predicting the intervention than growing a single tree in the original dataset. Machine learning algorithms using this approach of averaging trees include bagged trees and random forests (see, for instance, Ho, 1995; Breiman, 1996, 2001).

Another machine learning technique is called stepwise regression. This method utilizes a regression technique similar to the one discussed in chapter 3, section 3.2 to identify which characteristics significantly influence the outcome or intervention. The approach involves adding characteristics to the statistical model in sequence, beginning with the one that has the highest influence on the intervention (such as age in our previous example). In the next step, the characteristic with the highest influence among those characteristics that have not yet been included in the model is added, and so on. Similar to the decision tree, which consists of sequential data splits, stepwise regression consists of sequentially selecting characteristics in terms of how well they explain whether a subject receives or does not receive the intervention. And similar to decision trees, we can use (cross-)validation to find the number of characteristics that gives the highest accuracy for predicting the intervention.

There are more sophisticated regression methods available that, unlike stepwise regression, can partially account for the influence of characteristics instead of always fully including or excluding them from the model. It has been found that this partial accounting can lead to improved accuracy in predicting the intervention compared to using only the options of full inclusion or exclusion. Lasso and ridge regression are two examples of such sophisticated techniques, as for instance, discussed by Hoerl and Kennard (1970) and Tibshirani (1996). Also, in this context, we can use cross-validation to determine the optimal

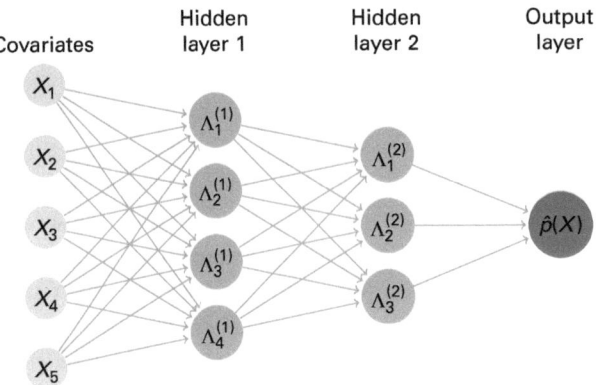

Figure 5.4
A neural network for treatment prediction

extent to which characteristics should be considered in the model to achieve the highest accuracy in predicting the intervention.

Neural networks are another machine learning approach that we will briefly introduce here, as discussed by McCulloch and Pitts (1943) and Ripley (1996). A neural network is a statistical model that consists not only of one but an entire system of regressions, with the aim being to achieve high accuracy in predicting the intervention or the outcome. Each characteristic serves as input to this system of regressions, which are connected and communicate with each other, a bit like the neurons in the human brain—hence the name "neural network." Including more regressions in the system increases its complexity and has a role similar to that of using more splits in a decision tree. Therefore, the question arises as to how many regressions (also known as "nodes") should be included in the neural network to maximize the accuracy of the prediction. Complex networks with many nodes that are organized in multiple layers are referred to as "deep learning" and are widely used in various domains, such as image classification (e.g., cats versus dogs) or natural language processing. Figure 5.4 provides an example of a neural network with five characteristics and two layers, one with four and the other with three nodes (or regressions, denoted by Λ), for estimating the model for the intervention. As with other machine learning approaches, validation can be used to help determine the optimal number of layers and nodes in the neural network to achieve the highest accuracy in predicting the intervention or outcome.

The final machine learning algorithm that we consider in our brief survey is the ensemble method. It consists of combining several machine learning algorithms by averaging their predictions (see, for instance, Zhou, 2012 and van der Laan et al., 2007). Such averaging may outperform each of the individual algorithms in terms of predictive accuracy. Also, for ensemble methods, we may use cross-validation to determine the optimal importance or weight of each algorithm in the average prediction, maximizing accuracy.

It is important to note that the machine learning algorithms we just discussed were originally developed for making predictions. For example, they can be used for churn analysis to identify which customers are most likely to switch their internet provider. However, such predictions are not useful for impact evaluation, as they typically cannot reveal the causal effect of an intervention. Predictive machine learning focuses solely on detecting patterns in how churn covaries with factors observed in the data. But such a covariance could occur for both causal and noncausal reasons, and predictive machine learning cannot distinguish between them. For instance, unobserved personal characteristics that affect both churn and the likelihood to receive a marketing intervention could make churn and the intervention covary (such that they tend to go up and down together), even though it is the unobserved characteristics that cause this movement. Nonetheless, predictive machine learning can serve as an ingredient in CML by providing models for the intervention and outcome, which can then be used for impact evaluation, for instance, based on DR expressions (chapter 4, equation (4.7)).

5.4 Effect Heterogeneity and Optimal Policy Learning

In section 5.2, our focus was on assessing the average impact of an intervention on a population, such as all customers. However, it is important to recognize that customers are not necessarily homogeneous in their responses to interventions. Some may respond more favorably to certain interventions than others, implying that the impact of an intervention is heterogeneous across individuals. In such cases, the average treatment effect (ATE) represents a combination of these heterogeneous effects. This concept is graphically illustrated in the upper part of figure 5.5 (which is inspired by a graph in Xie et al., 2018), where the ATE encompasses positive effects on some customers, negative effects on others, and potentially no discernible effect among a third group. For instance, consider a discount promotion: while it may increase net spending for some customers, it could decrease spending among others due to cannibalization effects. Meanwhile, a third group of customers might remain unaffected by the promotion.

Now imagine that we could use CML methods to determine whether some subgroups benefit more from an intervention than others. That is where the concept of effect heterogeneity analysis comes in—the idea of assessing how the impact of an intervention varies across different groups that can be described in terms of observed characteristics or covariates X. This concept is depicted in the lower part of figure 5.5, where subjects are categorized into subgroups based on the intervention's impact, such that the impact is heterogeneous across but homogeneous within subgroups. Indeed, in many business or organizational contexts, it appears relevant to know whether the impact varies significantly across subgroups like customer segments. Consider a scenario where a business analyst seeks to understand whether the impact of a new communication campaign varies across characteristics such as gender, age, education, or income. Identifying which groups, defined by observed characteristics,

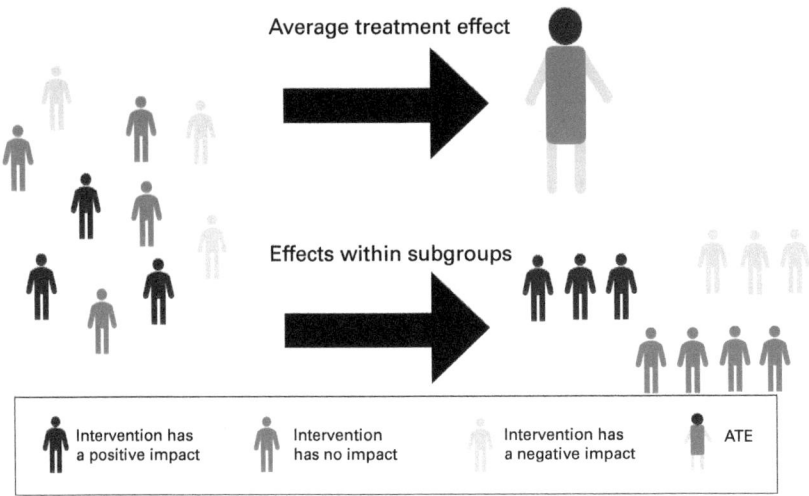

Figure 5.5
Average and heterogeneous effects

experience a notably high impact from the intervention, such as increased sales, can offer valuable insights for enhancing the intervention's effectiveness or cost efficiency. This also permits targeting of customer segments that exhibit a sufficiently large increase in sales after being exposed to the communication campaign in order to maximize the impact.

One CML approach for detecting effect heterogeneity is a modified version of a decision tree (as discussed in section 5.3). In this approach, the decision tree is used to predict not the intervention or outcome but, instead, the causal effect of the intervention on the outcome by recursively splitting the dataset based on characteristics X. By creating subgroups in which the impact of the intervention is as similar or homogeneous as possible, we at the same time create subgroups across which we have the highest heterogeneity in terms of the intervention's impact. In other words, the algorithm creates customer segments that are distinct in terms of the intervention's effect on the sales outcome, allowing us to differentiate between customer groups for whom the intervention is more or less effective in a data-driven manner. Therefore, the structure of the tree provides a definition of subgroups with the most heterogeneous causal effects up to a predefined number of splits.

This technique, known as a causal tree, was proposed by Athey and Imbens (2016) and can be used for both A/B tests (as discussed in chapter 3) and under a selection-on-observables assumption (when comparing apples with apples based on observed characteristics, as discussed in chapter 4). Analogous to the data-splitting approach outlined in section 5.2, the causal tree uses different parts of the data to perform different tasks—namely, to derive the splitting structure that maximizes effect heterogeneity across subsets and to estimate the treatment effects within the created subsets along with confidence intervals or p-values. This

Causal Machine Learning

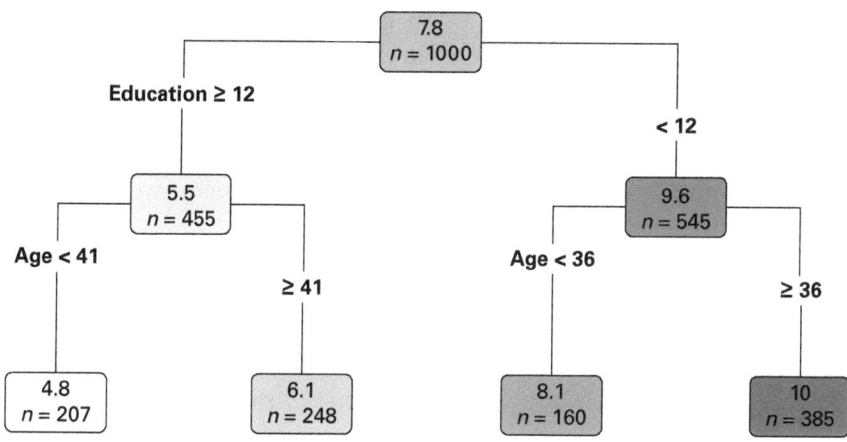

Figure 5.6
Causal tree

provides more honest assessments of the effect sizes than performing all tasks in the same dataset, as it avoids the previously discussed issue of overfitting bias.

Figure 5.6 shows an example of a causal tree that displays effect heterogeneity across customer segments, defined by characteristics where the intervention's impact differs the most. The top node of the tree represents the average treatment effect (ATE) of a marketing intervention in the total sample, which amounts to an increase in daily sales per customer of $7.8 on average. The information $n = 1,000$ indicates that the total sample consists of 1,000 customers. The effects of the intervention differ the most across customer segments with at least 12 years of education versus fewer years of education, and for this reason, the sample is split according to this value of education. Among the higher educated, the impact of the marketing intervention is $5.5, while it amounts to $9.6 among the less educated. Both customer segments are further divided into subsets based on age, which is another variable where the impact differs significantly. The causal tree ultimately consists of 4 different leaves or subsets of customers, across which the average impact ranges from $4.8 for the 207 customers with at least 12 years of education who are younger than 41 to $10 for the 385 customers with less than 12 years of education who are at least 36 years old.

Causal trees are not the only method for assessing effect heterogeneity—that is, how the impact varies across groups. Another approach is the causal (random) forest suggested by Wager and Athey (2018) and Athey et al. (2019), which averages over many causal trees (applied to many random subsamples of the data) to assess effect heterogeneity. Additionally, other machine learning methods such as lasso regression can be adapted for causal analysis such that they detect effect heterogeneity (see, for instance, Imai and Ratkovic, 2013). All these methods allow for the measurement of so-called individualized causal effects, which are the average effects among individuals who share the same values in observed characteristics (e.g., all individuals who are 36 years old and have 12 years of education). These effects are individualized in the sense that they do not represent the average effect for an entire population (such as all customers), but rather, represent the effect for a subset of subjects with specific values of characteristics X. This permits investigation of how the effects change across different values of the characteristics. Individualized effects are also known as conditional average treatment effects (CATEs) or conditional average causal effects, and are formally defined as

$$\Delta_x = E[Y(1) - Y(0)|X = x] \tag{5.1}$$

There are various ways to investigate how individualized effects differ across observed characteristics. The causal tree algorithm provides a splitting structure that informs us about the observed characteristics that mainly drive effect heterogeneity. However, with other algorithms, we cannot directly obtain this information from a tree structure. Nevertheless, we can still measure the importance of characteristics for effect heterogeneity. One option is to conduct a regression analysis (see chapter 3, section 3.2 for a brief discussion of regression). In this analysis, we model the individualized effect in equation (5.1) as a function of certain observed characteristics that appear interesting for assessing effect heterogeneity (see, e.g., the discussion in Semenova and Chernozhukov, 2021). For instance, we may be interested in determining whether the effect of a marketing intervention differs significantly between older and younger customers and, therefore, measure how the effect changes across age using regression.

As a real-world illustration, Huber et al. (2022) investigated the heterogeneity in the impact of discounts for train tickets on demand shifts, measured as rescheduling train trips, based on certain customer characteristics and travel purposes. These attributes include age, gender, travel distance, and the purpose of the trip (business or leisure). Their analysis reveals differences in the effect of discounts between leisure and business travelers, indicating that, holding other characteristics constant, a 1-percentage point increase in the discount rate leads to a 0.29 percentage point greater increase in rescheduled trips among leisure travelers than business travelers. This finding suggests that leisure travelers may demonstrate greater flexibility than business travelers in adjusting their travel schedules.

Another approach to investigate effect heterogeneity is to divide our data into categories with higher and lower individualized effects and examine whether the average values of specific or all characteristics differ significantly across these categories. For instance, we may find that the average age of customers is significantly higher in the category with the highest individualized effects than in categories with lower effects, suggesting variation in the impact of the intervention across age groups. Additionally, machine learning techniques can be used to identify the characteristics that are most predictive for the size of individualized effects in a data-driven manner. For example, we may model the individualized effects of a marketing campaign as a function of all observed characteristics using methods such as random forests or lasso regression and determine which characteristics predict the effects best. Huber et al. (2022) follow this approach, employing a random forest to predict individualized effects using various customer- or trip-related characteristics in the data. They find that demand-related characteristics such as seat capacity in trains, utilization, departure time, and distance are the most important predictors of effect size, with customer age also demonstrating some predictive power.

Assessing individualized effects is the foundation for optimally tailoring interventions to subgroups (defined by their observed characteristics), in which the intervention is most effective. This is known as optimal policy learning, which aims to optimally allocate a potentially costly intervention across subgroups based on their individualized effects' size (see, for instance, the discussion in Manski, 2004; Hirano and Porter, 2009; Dudík et al., 2011; and Kitagawa and Tetenov, 2018). In this decision-making process of optimal targeting, we can also take into account the intervention's costs, which may differ across subgroups based on their observed characteristics, such as geographical location. For example, a company may want to fine-tune its pricing strategy for their products or services to optimally target customers by offering discounts only to customer segments where the benefits, such as additional sales, outweigh the costs, such as reduced profit margins, on average. To define the customer segments, the company makes use of observed characteristics X, such as age, income, or education.

Using CML to learn the optimal targeting strategy from data can work well under certain conditions, similar to the estimation of average impacts such as the ATE. Even when the factors among all characteristics X that importantly affect both the intervention, such as pricing policy, and the outcome, such as sales, are unknown beforehand, CML can still identify the optimal targeting strategy. One condition for this is that machine learning models successfully learn which characteristics importantly drive the intervention and the outcome, which is likely if the number of important characteristics is not too large relative to the number of subjects in our database. Another condition is that the number of potential subgroups, or customer segments, that should be targeted by the intervention (or not) is not excessively large. This condition is, for instance, satisfied if we predefine a limited number of policy choices about which subgroups or customer segments are targeted by the intervention. For instance, possible policy choices could include offering discounts to either more or less frequent buyers or to either previous or new customers. The algorithm then aims to learn the optimal allocation of the intervention from these choices.

Rather than maximizing benefits by allocating predefined policy rules to predefined customer segments, we can take a more sophisticated approach and learn both the optimal customer segmentation and the optimal intervention assignment for each segment in a data-driven way. In this case, we only need to define the number of customer segments to create in the process of finding the optimal targeting strategy, but neither the definition of the segments nor the possible policy choices per segment need to be specified beforehand. This algorithm, which learns optimal intervention policies across a fixed number of a priori unknown customer segments, is called a policy tree (see Athey and Wager, 2021). It is

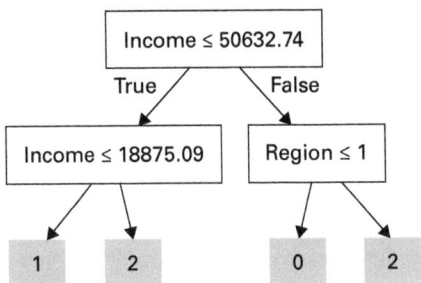

Figure 5.7
Policy tree for a marketing intervention

related to, but different from, the previously mentioned causal tree. The policy tree uses a statistic that is related to the individualized effect (i) to optimally split the data (i.e., group subjects in the data) into segments according to observed characteristics that affect the individualized effects and (ii) to assign (possibly distinct) interventions to the various subgroups in a way that maximizes the overall effect. Therefore, the policy tree yields optimal intervention rules for the various subgroups that can be intuitively described by the tree structure of how the data are split.

Figure 5.7 illustrates a policy tree example where a marketing intervention is optimally allocated across four customer segments based on observed customer characteristics. The marketing intervention is denoted by the values 0 (no intervention), 1 (small discount), and 2 (large discount) and should maximize the net benefits per customer (accounting for the granted discount within overall spending). The segmentation into these four groups is initially unknown but is optimally determined through data-driven analysis. The algorithm generates customer segments based on the characteristics "annual income" and "region," identified as the most suitable criteria for optimally targeting customers. According to the algorithm, customers with an income below $18,875.10 should receive a small discount (1), while those earning between $18,875.10 and $50,632.74 should obtain a larger discount (2) to maximize net benefits. For individuals earning $50,632.75 dollars or more, those in region 1 should not receive any discount (0), as discounts do not seem to increase net benefits in this specific region. However, in other regions, such higher-income customers should receive a larger discount (2) to optimize net benefits.

5.5 Use Cases in R

Let's consider an application of double machine learning (DML), as discussed in section 5.2 using the statistical software R. To do this, we first load the previously considered *causalweight* package using the *library* command and then use the *coupon* dataset, which contains information on the receipt of coupons and customer spending. We define the outcome

Causal Machine Learning

variable as *y*, the intervention variable as *d*, and the covariates as *x*, in the same way as we did in chapter 4, section 4.4. We can do this by running the following commands: *y* = *coupon[,1]*; *d* = *coupon[,2]*; *x* = *as.matrix(coupon[,3:9])*. Next, we run the *treatDML* command for DML, using the outcome, intervention, and covariates as the first, second, and third arguments, respectively. By default, this DML procedure applies lasso regression for estimating the propensity scores and conditional mean outcomes. We store the results in a variable called *results* and inspect the average treatment effect (ATE) estimate and the *p*-value by calling the *results$effect* and *results$pval* objects. The box below provides the R code for each step.

```
library(causalweight)                                    # load causalweight package
data(coupon)                                             # load coupon data
y=coupon[,1]; d=coupon[,2]; x=as.matrix(coupon[,3:9])    # define variables
results=treatDML(y=y, d=d, x=x)                          # run DML with lasso
results$effect; results$pval;                            # show impact and p-value
```

Running the code yields the following output.

```
[1] 62.58773
[1] 0.00686087
```

The ATE estimate obtained using DML is $62.58, which indicates a positive effect of the coupon campaign on sales, consistent with the findings in chapter 4, section 4.4. The *p*-value is very small (0.68%), implying that the chance of the ATE being zero in the entire customer population, despite finding a clearly nonzero effect in our database, is less than 1%.

Next, we estimate individualized effects or CATEs using the causal forest approach discussed in section 5.4. To do this, we first install and load the *grf* package. We then use the *causalforest* command, where the first argument, *X*, corresponds to the covariates, the second argument, *Y*, to the outcome, and the third argument, *W*, to the intervention. Therefore, we run the command *causalforest(X=x, Y=y, W=d)* and save the results in an R object named *results*. The predicted CATEs for all customers in our data are stored in a subobject called *predictions*. We can access this subobject using the code *results$predictions*. By wrapping the latter with the histogram command *hist*, we can inspect the distribution of CATEs in our customer database. The following box provides the R code for the various steps.

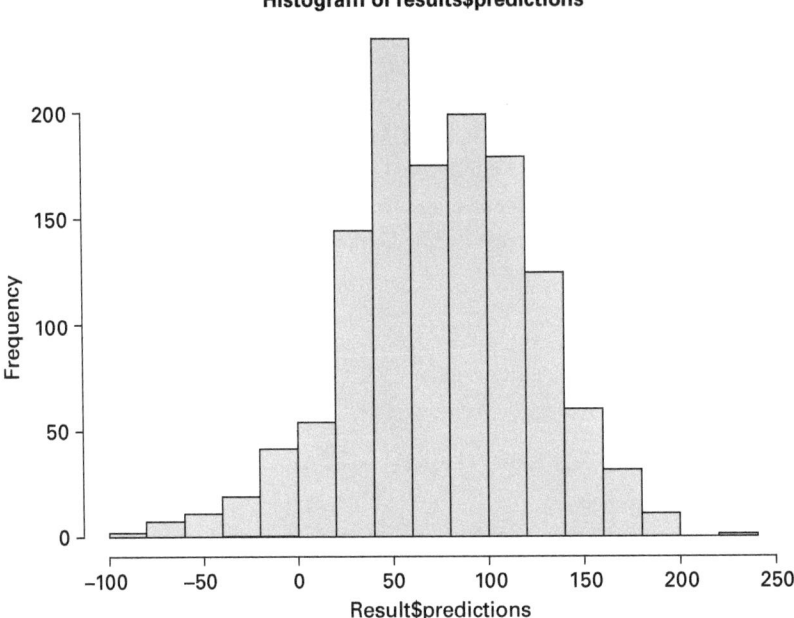

Figure 5.8
CATEs

```
install.packages("grf")                    # install package
library(grf)                               # load grf package
results=causal_forest(X=x, Y=y, W=d)       # run causal forest
hist(results$predictions)                  # distribution of CATEs
```

Running the provided code generates the graph shown in figure 5.8, which displays the distribution of CATEs. The y-axis shows the frequency of different CATE values, while the x-axis shows the actual CATE values for the customers in our dataset. The graph highlights that the CATEs may vary substantially across customers with different background characteristics X, indicating significant heterogeneity in the effectiveness of the coupon campaign. For the majority of customers, we predict the impact to lie between $20 and $150, given their background characteristics X (such as previous purchases and so on). However, for some customers, the expected effect is lower or even negative, while for a few others, it exceeds $200

Next, we want to investigate whether the CATEs differ significantly across one customer characteristic of particular interest: previous spending prior to receiving a coupon. This allows us to assess whether and how the impact of the coupon campaign depends on customer loyalty, as measured by the volume of customers' previous purchases. To do so, we use the *bestlinearprojection* command and provide its first argument, *forest*, with the output from the causal forest (*results*). For the second argument, denoted by A, we specify $x[,2]$, which corresponds to the second column of the covariate matrix X and represents the customer's daily spending in the previous period. The following box provides the R code.

```
best_linear_projection(forest=results,A=x[,2])    # CATEs by past spending
```

Running this code yields the following output.

```
Estimate Std. Error t value Pr(>|t|)
(Intercept) 61.21840    35.89560  1.7055  0.08835 .
A1           0.11819     0.07232  1.6343  0.10245

---
Signif. codes:  0 '***' 0.001 '**' 0.01 '*' 0.05 '.' 0.1 ' ' 1
```

The results suggest that for each additional dollar spent in the previous period, the effect of coupon receipt increases by roughly $0.12 in the period when the coupons are issued. This indicates that the coupon campaign is more effective among loyal customers who spent comparatively more prior to the campaign. However, the *p*-value is 10.24%, which is not statistically significant at the 5% level. This implies that when claiming that impact size differs across previous spending, we face a risk higher than 5% that there is actually no true association between the impact and loyalty in the population of all customers.

Next, we aim to detect those characteristics that are most informative (or predictive) about the size of the CATE in a data-driven way using a random forest. To do this, we run the *regression forest* command, where we set the first argument X to our characteristics x and the second argument Y to our estimated CATEs *results$predictions*. That is, we predict the size of the CATEs using the customer characteristics. We store the results in an R object named *heterogeneity*. Finally, we use the *variable_importance* command to investigate the importance of the various characteristics in X for predicting the CATE. This allows us to determine which characteristics are most informative for characterizing the impact of coupons on sales. The box below provides the R code for the various steps.

```
heterogeneity=regression_forest(X=x, Y=results$predictions)   # CATE predicted by x
variable_importance(heterogeneity)                            # predictive importance
```

Running the code gives the output below, which shows the importance of each characteristic in predicting the size of the CATE. The importance is calculated as a weighted sum of how often a characteristic is used for splitting at each splitting decision in the forest.

```
[1,] 0.003513918
[2,] 0.712393160
[3,] 0.046812815
[4,] 0.054443336
[5,] 0.008630863
[6,] 0.004152127
[7,] 0.170053781
```

We observe that the second characteristic—that is, previous customer spending, is by far the most important predictor of the heterogeneity in the impact of the coupon campaign. The second most important characteristic is the seventh covariate—that is, family size. The remaining characteristics do not appear to be significant predictors of the impact of the intervention.

Finally, we implement policy learning for optimally assigning coupons or no coupons to different customer segments that are determined in a data-driven way. We begin by installing and loading the *policytree* and *DiagrammeR* packages, which contain the commands for policy learning and the procedures for creating diagrams and graphs, respectively. We then use the *multi_arm_causal forest* command to estimate the propensity score model for the intervention and the conditional mean outcomes using random forests. In the command, the first argument (X) corresponds to the covariates, which we set to x. The second argument (Y) corresponds to the outcome, which we set to y. The third argument (W) corresponds to the intervention, which must be coded as a nonnumeric variable in a data format called a factor. To account for this, we wrap our intervention by the *factor* command when defining it to be

Causal Machine Learning

the third argument: *multi_arm_causal_forest(X=x, Y=y, W=factor(d))*. We save the results in an R object called *forest*. Next, we use the *double_robust_scores* command to calculate the DR functions necessary for policy learning, using the *forest* object as input. We save these functions in another R object, called *dr*.

Next, we use the *policy_tree* command to simultaneously perform data-driven customer segmentation and the optimal assignment of interventions within customer segments. Its first argument (X) corresponds to the characteristics based on which the customers should be optimally segmented and the intervention should be optimally assigned, which we set to x. The second argument (*Gamma*) corresponds to the DR functions, which are stored in our *dr* object. The third argument (*depth*) defines the number of customer segments we want to obtain, in terms of powers of 2. For example, setting *depth=1* implies $2^1 = 2$ customer segments, while *depth=2* entails $2^2 = 4$ segments, and *depth=3* $2^3 = 8$ segments. We set *depth=2* and store the results in an R object called *tree*, which contains our policy tree with optimally assigned interventions. Finally, we plot the policy tree using the *plot* command with the *tree* object as input. In the *plot* command, we also set the argument *leaf.labels=levels(factor(d))*, so that the labeling of the optimal policies suggested for the various customer segments corresponds to the labeling of our intervention variable—namely, 1 or 0. The code for the various steps is provided in the box below.

```
install.packages("policytree", "DiagrammeR")      # install packages
library(policytree)                                # load policytree package
library(DiagrammeR)                                # load DiagrammeR package
forest=multi_arm_causal_forest(X=x, Y=y, W=factor(d))  # treatment+outcome models
dr=double_robust_scores(forest)                    # DR functions
tree=policy_tree(X=x, Gamma=dr, depth=2)           # policies for 4 subgroups
plot(tree, leaf.labels=levels(factor(d)))          # tree with optimal policy
```

Running the code gives the policy tree depicted in figure 5.9. We see that the optimal customer segmentation is based on first splitting the database into customers previously spending at most $158.31 versus more than $158.31. The subset of customers who previously spent less is further divided into two subgroups based on family size: those with a family size of four or less and those with more members. Similarly, the subset of customers who previously spent more than $158.31 is divided into two subgroups: those who spent up to $238.87 and those who spent more than $238.87. The policy tree's lowest four boxes contain recommendations on which interventions to assign to various customer

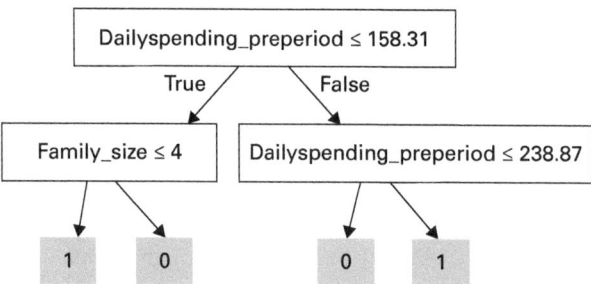

Figure 5.9
Policy tree in R

segments, making it a useful tool to visualize which segments should be targeted by the coupon campaign according to the algorithm. For customers who previously spent at most $158.31 and have a family size of four or less, the optimal policy is 1—that is, providing coupons. However, for those who previously spent at most $158.31 but have larger families, the optimal policy is 0—that is, no coupons. The same no-coupon policy applies to those who previously spent more than $158.31 but up to $238.87, while those who spent more than $238.87 dollars should receive coupons.

5.6 Use Cases in Python

This section implements causal machine learning in Python, addressing the same use cases covered in section 5.5 using R. To estimate the ATE of receiving coupons on customer spending using double machine learning (DML), we load the *doubleml* library alongside the *pandas* library and the *linear_model* module from the *sklearn* library. Following the steps outlined in the final Python use case in chapter 4, section 4.5, we create a data object named *dml_data* from the coupon data, where the outcome, intervention, and covariates are defined. In the next step, we specify the outcome model ml_l to be estimated by linear lasso regression (*LassoCV model*) and the intervention model ml_m to be estimated by logistic lasso regression (*LogisticRegressionCV model* with '*l1*' as penalty term).

We feed the data and lasso machine learners into the *DoubleMLPLR* procedure and run the *fit()* command to estimate the ATE, where *n_folds=3* implies cross-fitting with three subsamples (or folds). We save the output in an object named *dml_lasso*. Finally, we use the *print* command to display the *summary* attribute of the *dml_lasso* object. The estimated ATE suggests that coupon receipt increases daily customer spending on average by $55.70, somewhat lower than the corresponding R-based estimate in the first use case of section 5.5, but not drastically different. Furthermore, the *p*-value is very close to zero. The Python code for each step is provided in the box below.

```
import pandas as pd                                      # load pandas library
import doubleml as dml                                   # load doubleml library
from sklearn import linear_model                         # load from sklearn
df = pd.read_csv('data/coupon.csv')                      # load coupon data
X = df.drop(['dailyspending', 'coupons'], axis = 1)      # define covariates
dml_data = dml.DoubleMLData(df,                          # create data
    y_col = 'dailyspending',                             # define outcome
    d_cols = 'coupons',                                  # define intervention
    x_cols = list(X.columns.values))                     # define covariates
ml_l = linear_model.LassoCV()                            # learner for outcome
ml_m = linear_model.LogisticRegressionCV(penalty = 'l1', # learner for treatment
    solver = 'saga',                                     # solver
    max_iter = 350,                                      # max. iterations
    Cs = 1,                                              # inverse regularization
    tol = 0.01)                                          # tolerance for stopping
dml_lasso = dml.DoubleMLPLR(dml_data,                    # double machine learning
    ml_l,                                                # outcome model
    ml_m,                                                # treatment model
    n_folds = 3).fit()                                   # number of folds
print(dml_lasso.summary)                                 # show the results
```

Next, we estimate individualized effects or CATEs based on the causal forest. To achieve this, we import the *GRFForestCausalRegressor* module from the *skgrf* library and load the *pandas* and *matplotlib* libraries. After loading the coupon data into a Pandas data frame, we convert column names to strings using the *columns.astype(str)* command. Next, we define the outcome variable Y as *dailyspending*, the intervention D as *coupons*, and the covariates X to correspond to the remaining columns of the data. The causal forest is set up using the *GRFForestCausalRegressor* command with the option *enable_tree_details=True* to include details of the algorithm. We implement the causal forest in the data using the *fit(X = X, y = Y, w = D)* command, where *w* denotes the intervention. Then, the CATEs are computed using the *predict(X)* function, which uses the covariate values X observed in our data to estimate the CATE for each customer. Next, we generate a histogram of the CATEs using the *plt.hist* command and then label the axes. Finally, we display the histogram, visualizing the distribution of estimated treatment effects, with the *plt.show()* command. The distribution of CATEs is very similar to the histogram obtained through R in the second use case of section 5.5, as illustrated in figure 5.8. The Python code for each step is provided in the box below.

```python
from skgrf.ensemble import GRFForestCausalRegressor    # load CausalForest
import pandas as pd                                    # load pandas library
import matplotlib.pyplot as plt                        # load matplotlib library
df = pd.read_csv('data/coupon.csv')                    # load coupon data
df.columns = df.columns.astype(str)                    # convert column names
Y = df['dailyspending']                                # define outcome
D = df['coupons']                                      # define intervention
X = df.drop(['dailyspending', 'coupons'], axis = 1)    # define covariates
cf = GRFForestCausalRegressor(enable_tree_details=True) # set up causal forest
cf.fit(X = X, y = Y, w = D)                            # fit causal forest
CATE = cf.predict(X)                                   # compute CATEs
plt.hist(CATE, color = 'gray', bins = 16, rwidth = 0.9) # plot histogram of CATEs
plt.xlabel('Predictions')                              # set xlabel
plt.ylabel('Frequency')                                # set ylabel
plt.title('Histogram of predictions')                  # set title
plt.show()                                             # show plot
```

In our next Python example, we apply double machine learning (DML) to explore potential variations or heterogeneity in the impact of coupons based on customers' previous spending. Initially, we load the required libraries—*pandas*, *numpy*, and *doubleml*—along with the *ensemble* module from *sklearn* for machine learning models. Following the methodology outlined in the final Python use case in chapter 4, section 4.5, we create a data object named *dml_data* from the coupon data, specifying the outcome, intervention, and covariates. Subsequently, we define the outcome model (*ml_g*) to be estimated using a random forest for regression (*RandomForestRegressor*), suitable for outcomes with multiple values such as spending. The intervention model (*ml_m*) is defined using a random forest for classification (*RandomForestClassifier*), suitable for variables that take values 1 or 0. Employing the *DoubleMLIRM* procedure with the *.fit()* command, we execute DML on our data, incorporating specific options such as a trimming rule for excluding observations with extreme propensity scores. The results are stored in an object named *est*.

Following this, we introduce a constant term named *intercept* to the data and define a subset (*cateX*) comprising the *intercept* and the variable *dailyspending_preperiod*, which we use to explore the heterogeneity of the coupon impact. We apply the *cate* command to *cateX* and save the results in an object named *CATEs*. Finally, we use the *print* command to inspect the results, revealing that for each additional dollar spent in the previous period, the effect of coupon receipt increases by approximately $0.17. This estimate is slightly higher than the $0.12 increase obtained from the R-based analysis in the third use case of section 5.5, as the Python and R implementations of the method are not fully equivalent. The *p*-value is 0.255, suggesting that when claiming a difference in impact size across previous spending based on our estimates, we face a nonnegligible risk that there is in reality no association between previous spending and the size of the effect. This *p*-value is even larger than the 10.24% obtained in the R-based analysis. The corresponding Python code is provided in the following box.

```
import pandas as pd                                          # load pandas library
import numpy as np                                           # load numpy library
import doubleml as dml                                       # load doubleml library
from sklearn import ensemble                                 # load ensemble from sklearn
df = pd.read_csv('data/coupon.csv')                          # load coupon data
X = df.drop(['dailyspending', 'coupons'], axis = 1)          # select covariates
dml_data = dml.DoubleMLData(df,                              # create data
    y_col = 'dailyspending',                                 # define outcome
    d_cols = 'coupons',                                      # define intervention
    x_cols = list(X.columns.values))                         # define covariates
ml_g = ensemble.RandomForestRegressor(max_features = 'sqrt') # outcome model
ml_m = ensemble.RandomForestClassifier()                     # intervention model
est = dml.DoubleMLIRM(dml_data,                              # double machine learning
    ml_g,                                                    # learner for outcome
    ml_m,                                                    # learner for intervention
    normalize_ipw = True,                                    # normalize weights
    trimming_rule = 'truncate',                              # trimming approach
    trimming_threshold = 0.01).fit()                         # threshold for trimming
df['intercept'] = np.ones(len(df))                           # create constant
cateX = df.loc[:, ['intercept', 'dailyspending_preperiod']]  # X for heterogeneity
CATEs = est.cate(cateX)                                      # estimate effect heterogeneity
print(CATEs)                                                 # CATEs by past spending
```

Next, we investigate which characteristics (or covariates) are most predictive about the size of the CATE in a data-driven way with a random forest using the *GRFForestRegressor* command, which we import from the *skgrf* library. We utilize the *GRFForestRegressor* command from the *skgrf* library for a random forest analysis. The *fit(X = X, y = CATE)* command is used to predict the CATEs (*CATE*), previously estimated in the second use case of this chapter, based on customer characteristics (X). We store the results in an object named *heterogeneity* and then employ the *get_feature_importances* command, which reveals the predictive importance of each characteristic in determining the heterogeneity of treatment effects. While the numerical values of importance differ from those obtained through the R procedure in the fourth use case of section 5.5 (due to variations in the methods for computing importance), the results are qualitatively similar. Notably, the second characteristic, previous customer spending, emerges as the most important predictor of heterogeneity in the impact of coupons, followed by the seventh covariate, family size. The Python code for each step is provided in the box below.

```
from skgrf.ensemble import GRFForestRegressor         # import ForestRegressor
heterogeneity = GRFForestRegressor().fit(X = X, y = CATE)  # CATE predicted by X
heterogeneity.get_feature_importances()               # predictive importance X
```

In our concluding use case, we delve into policy learning to determine the optimal assignment of coupons to distinct customer segments. In pursuit of this, we utilize the *policy_tree* command on the *est* object, which encapsulates the output from the double machine learning (DML) procedure conducted in the third use case of this chapter. In the command, we specify *features = X*, signifying that optimal segmentation of customers should be based on all available customer characteristics. Additionally, we set *depth = 2*, implying the creation of $2^2 = 4$ customer segments, mirroring the approach in the R-based example from the previous chapter. We save the results in an object named *policy_tree*. Subsequently, the *plot_tree()* command is executed to visually represent the policy tree, enabling the examination of the optimal intervention assignments within the identified subgroups. The Python code for this task is presented in the box below.

```
policy_tree = est.policy_tree(features = X, depth = 2)  # policies for 4 subgroups
policy_tree.plot_tree()                                 # tree with optimal policy
```

Running the code yields the policy tree displayed in figure 5.10. Compared to the R-based use case at the end of the section 5.5, the customer segmentation looks different.

In this Python-based policy tree, the segmentation is determined by family size, age, and income. For instance, customers with a family size of five or more and falling within

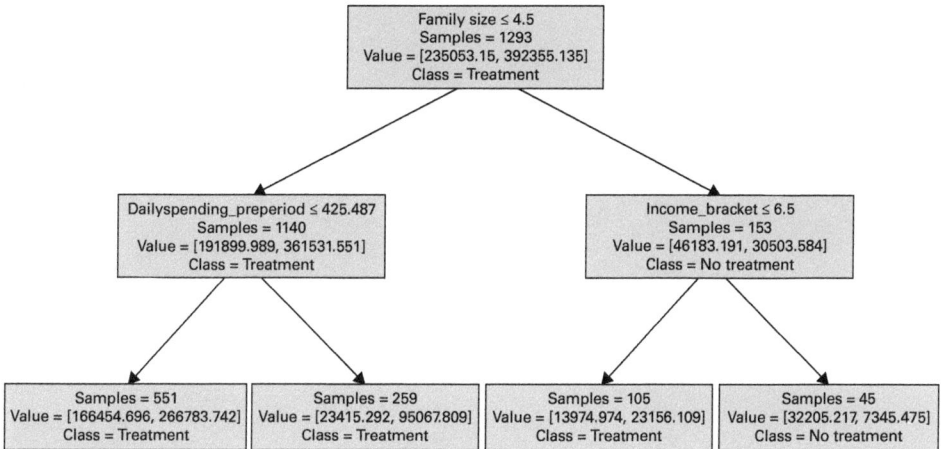

Figure 5.10
Policy tree in Python

an income bracket of seven or more are recommended not to receive the intervention; see the box located at the lower right of the policy tree. In contrast, the R-based policy tree in the previous section constructed customer segments based on family size and previous spending. These disparities arise from the nonequivalence of the Python and R methods, potentially resulting in different customer segmentations, especially in cases where multiple segmentations could yield similar results in terms of effectiveness.

6 Instrumental Variables

6.1 Instruments and Complier Effects

In Chapter 4, we discussed the selection-on-observables assumption for impact evaluation. However, this assumption fails to hold if the subjects receiving and not receiving an intervention differ in unobserved characteristics that also affect the outcome, even after controlling for observed characteristics. Let's consider an example: a bank runs an experimental evaluation by randomly offering financial consultations to some customers but not to others in order to study the effect of these consultations on savings plans. But here is the catch: some customers who receive the offer do not comply, in the sense that they do not actually take up or receive the consultation, meaning they miss out on the intervention. This is known as imperfect compliance. The decision to forego the consultation could be influenced by unobserved factors like interest in financial issues, motivation, and financial literacy. If these factors also affect the outcome—that is, savings plan decisions, then comparing the savings plans of customers who received the consultation with those who did not would not accurately measure the impact of the consultation. The experiment is no longer valid because the decision not to comply with the offer jeopardizes the comparability of customers with and without the intervention. It is like comparing apples and oranges.

Is it possible to salvage any useful information from our broken experiment and evaluate the impact of the intervention? The answer is a tentative "yes," provided that certain behavioral assumptions hold for a subgroup of the customers targeted by our experiment. The first assumption is that the offer of financial consultation should only affect savings outcomes through the actual receipt of consultation. This excludes any direct impact of the offer on the outcome other than through its impact on receiving the intervention, which is known as exclusion restriction. The latter would, for instance, be violated if the mere offer of consultation induced some customers to save more by increasing the salience or attention paid to financial issues, even without receiving consultation. A second assumption is that the instrument is not influenced by any (possibly unobserved) characteristics that might also affect the outcome. For instance, in our experiment, receiving an offer for financial consultation should ideally be random and unaffected by customer characteristics like interest.

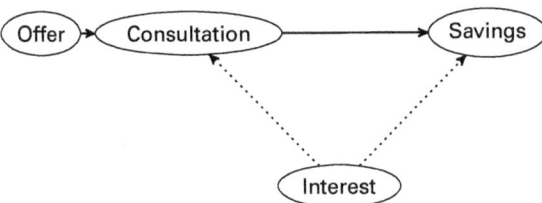

Figure 6.1
A random offer as instrument for financial consultation

A third assumption is that the offer of intervention induces at least some people to actually take it, who thus comply with the offer, while not discouraging the take-up for anyone else. For example, some customers, the so-called compliers, may be motivated by the offer to receive consultation, while for others, the receipt of consultation is unaffected by the offer. However, the offer should not discourage anyone from taking up the intervention. Such discouragement would occur if some customers were planning to take up consultation even without the offer but were then discouraged from doing so when they received an offer, due to their suspicion about marketing activities. Ruling out such discouragement, which means ruling out the possibility that the random offer can reduce the take-up of the intervention, is known as the weak monotonicity assumption. This implies that discouraged and encouraged subjects may not exist at the same time (while subjects unaffected by the offer may exist).

Figure 6.1 presents a causal graph depicting this scenario. The offering of consultation does not directly impact the savings outcome except through the actual receipt of financial consultation. Furthermore, the offer is not influenced by a customer's interest in financial issues due to its experimental or random assignment (while interest might affect receipt of consultation and savings decisions). Moreover, it is essential that the offer causally affects the receipt of consultation for at least some customers, serving as encouragement—inducing certain customers to opt for consultation—while never acting as a discouragement for any customer.

Under these assumptions, we can apply a technique known as an instrumental variable approach, which was first formulated by Wright (1928) and more recently discussed by Imbens and Angrist (1994) and Angrist et al. (1996). In this approach, the random offer is considered an "instrument" for measuring the effect of the intervention by using a mathematical trick. The trick is based on the fact that, by the exclusion restriction and monotonicity assumption, any impact of the random offer on the outcome operates exclusively through the offer's effect on the take-up of the intervention among compliers. Therefore, we can calculate the average effect of the intervention on the outcome among the subgroup of compliers by scaling (or dividing) the average impact of the random offer on the outcome by the average impact of the offer on the actual receipt of the intervention.

To give an example, assume that the average effect of the offer on the outcome is $1,000; that is, savings go up by $1,000 dollars on average when consultation is offered. Furthermore, the average effect of the random offer on the intervention is 0.5, or 50%; that is, 50% of customers are compliers, because the offer induces them to take consultation. It follows that the impact among compliers is 1,000/0.5 = $2,000. Scaling the effect of the offer on the outcome by the effect of the offer on intervention accounts for the fact that only compliers contribute to the effect of the offer on the outcome (because other groups do not react in terms of their intervention). This allows us to estimate the impact of the intervention among compliers, which is commonly referred to as complier average causal effect (CACE) or local average treatment effect (LATE). The effect is local in the sense that it refers only to the subgroup of compliers, rather than the entire population.

As another example, let's consider a situation where a company introduces a new customer loyalty program, offering exclusive discounts and rewards to members. The average effect of the loyalty program on customer spending is estimated to be a $100 increase in purchases. However, only 25% of customers enroll in the loyalty program, indicating that 25% are compliers who were enticed by the offer to join the program. To estimate the LATE, we scale the effect of the loyalty program on average spending per customer by the effect of the offer on enrollment. In this case, the impact among compliers is $100/0.25 = 400$. This implies that among those who were influenced by the offer to enroll in the loyalty program (the compliers), their spending increased by an average of $400. See, for instance, Ebbes et al. (2017) for more examples of instrument-based impact evaluation in the domain of marketing.

6.2 Behavioral Assumptions and Methods

To discuss the instrumental variable approach more formally, let's denote by Z the random offer of an intervention, where $Z=1$ if someone receives the offer and $Z=0$ if they do not. Similar to the potential outcome notation used so far, we $D(1)$ and $D(0)$ represent the potential intervention if the instrument $Z=1$ and $Z=0$, respectively, while potential outcomes $Y(1)$ and $Y(0)$ are defined in terms of intervention states $D=1$ and $D=0$. The behavioral assumptions discussed in the previous section 6.1 can then be stated as follows:

$$\{D(1), D(0), Y(1), Y(0)\} \perp Z, \tag{6.1}$$

$$\Pr(D(1) \geq D(0)) = 100\%, \quad E[D|Z=1] - E[D|Z=0] \neq 0.$$

The first line of expression (6.1) presents the instrument validity assumption, which consists of two conditions. The first condition is that the instrument Z is independent of the potential intervention and outcome states, such that there are no characteristics that jointly affect Z, on one hand, and intervention D and/or outcome Y, on the other hand. This condition is satisfied by design if Z is randomly assigned, such as in the case of randomly offering consultations. This is similar to the independence condition in expression (3.1) in chapter 3, section 3.2,

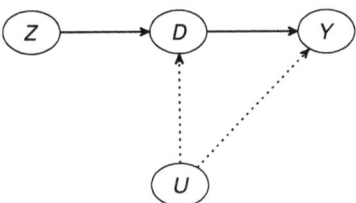

Figure 6.2
An instrumental variable approach

which was, however, imposed with respect to the intervention D rather than the instrument Z. The second condition is that the instrument Z does not directly affect the outcome Y other than through intervention D, which is the exclusion restriction previously mentioned. This is implicit in our potential outcome notation, as $Y(1)$ and $Y(0)$ are only defined in terms of intervention D, and not additionally in terms of instrument Z.

Figure 6.2 presents a framework that satisfies instrument validity, as there are no unobserved characteristics that jointly affect the instrument Z and the outcome Y. This implies that the instrument is (as good as) random. Additionally, the exclusion restriction is met, as Z only affects Y through the intervention D. In contrast to the instrument, the intervention may, however, be affected by unobserved characteristics, denoted by U, which also influence Y. The causal effects of U are represented by dotted arrows, highlighting that they cannot be measured because U is unobserved.

The second line of expression (6.1) contains two more conditions that are critical for identifying the causal effect of the intervention using the instrumental variable. The first condition, $\Pr(D(1) \geq D(0)) = 100\%$, specifies that offering the instrument (such as consultation) either increases the take-up of the intervention (i.e., $D(1) > D(0)$) or has no effect on it (i.e., $D(1) = D(0)$). However, providing the instrument cannot decrease the take-up of the intervention (i.e., $D(1) < D(0)$), which was discussed in terms of the monotonicity assumption in section 6.1. This assumption is automatically satisfied when it is impossible to receive the intervention without the instrument. For instance, if you cannot access a consultation without being offered it first, then monotonicity holds. The second expression in the second line, $E[D|Z=1] - E[D|Z=0] \neq 0$, means that the average impact of the instrument on the intervention is not zero. Monotonicity and this expression together imply the existence of compliers—that is, of individuals who are induced to take the intervention if provided with the instrument, $D(1) > D(0)$. Under our behavioral assumptions and a binary intervention D that is only 1 or 0, the difference $E[D|Z=1] - E[D|Z=0]$ corresponds to the share of compliers in the population.

The assumptions in expression (6.1) allow us to identify the LATE on the compliers, which is formally defined as the difference between the expected outcome if all compliers received the intervention and the expected outcome if all compliers did not receive the intervention, denoted as

$$\Delta_{D(1)=1,D(0)=0} = E[Y(1) - Y(0)|D(1) = 1, D(0) = 0]. \qquad (6.2)$$

Under the assumptions in expression (6.1), the LATE corresponds to the ratio of the average impact of instrument Z on the outcome Y, $E[Y|Z=1] - E[Y|Z=0]$, known as the intention to treat or reduced form effect, and the average impact of the instrument Z on the intervention D, $E[D|Z=1] - E[D|Z=0]$, known as first-stage effect. Formally, we can express the LATE as follows (see, for instance, Wald, 1940):

$$\Delta_{D(1)=1,D(0)=0} = \frac{E[Y|Z=1] - E[Y|Z=0]}{E[D|Z=1] - E[D|Z=0]}. \qquad (6.3)$$

Another approach that can be used to estimate the average impact of the intervention among compliers involves a two-stage regression approach (see chapter 3, section 3.2 for a discussion of regression). In this approach, we first estimate a linear regression of intervention D on a constant and instrument Z (the first stage regression), and then estimate a linear regression of outcome Y on a constant and the predicted intervention from the first stage (i.e., $E[D|Z]$). The two-stage regression approach is numerically equivalent to using equation (6.3) to estimate the LATE.

It may not always be plausible to assume that instrumental variable assumptions like random assignment hold unconditionally—that is, without making the groups receiving the instrument ($Z=1$) and those not receiving the instrument ($Z=0$) comparable in terms of observed covariates X. Similar to the discussion in chapter 4 (which, however, was with respect to the intervention D rather than the instrument Z), we would be comparing apples with oranges if the groups differed in terms of characteristics that also affect the outcome. Imagine a scenario where a bank's management is trying to improve the bank's positioning among female customers. As a result, female customers are more likely to receive invitations than male customers. Therefore, the share of offer recipients is higher among females than males, making the offer nonrandom with respect to gender. However, it may still be plausible to assume that the offer is random within gender—that is, when only comparing females with females or males with males (i.e., apples with apples).

In cases where we can account for all characteristics that jointly affect the instrument Z and the outcome Y based on observed covariates X, we can implement the instrument approach by controlling for these covariates. This involves making groups with $Z=1$ and $Z=0$ comparable in covariates X, which modifies expression (6.1) to hold conditional on X (see, for instance, Abadie, 2003):

$$\{D(1), D(0), Y(1), Y(1)\} \perp Z | X, \qquad (6.4)$$

$$\Pr(D(1) \geq D(0)|X) = 100\%, \quad E[D|Z=1, X] - E[D|Z=0, X] \neq 0,$$

$$0\% < P(Z=1|X) < 100\%.$$

The first line of the modified expression (6.4) requires that instrument validity holds conditional on X, meaning the instrument is as good as randomly assigned and satisfies the

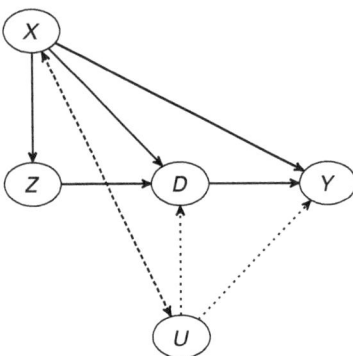

Figure 6.3
An instrumental variable approach with covariates

exclusion restriction among observations with the same covariate values. The second line assumes monotonicity of D in Z and the existence of compliers conditional on X. The third line is a common support restriction on the instrument propensity score $\Pr(Z=1|X)$, implying that subjects with both $Z=1$ and $Z=0$ exist for all covariate values X. Figure 6.3 presents a framework that satisfies the instrument validity assumption conditional on X. It depicts the possibility that unobservable factors U may affect X or be influenced by X, as indicated by the bidirectional dotted arrow, or that both U and X may be influenced by additional unobservable factors. However, given X, no unobservable factor may jointly affect both the instrument Z and the outcome Y.

We can think of the assumption $D(1), D(0), Y(1), Y(1) \perp Z|X$ in expression (6.4) as a selection-of-observables assumption, similar to the one in chapter 4, but now regarding the instrument rather than the intervention. Therefore, we can measure the effect of instrument Z on outcome Y or intervention D when controlling for covariates X, just as we measured the impact of intervention D on outcome Y when controlling for X in chapter 4. We can replace D with Z and the propensity score on the intervention, $\Pr(D=1|X)$, with the instrument propensity score $\Pr(Z=1|X)$ in any expression for the ATE, such as in equation (4.3), (4.5), or (4.7), to obtain the intention-to-treat (ITT) effect of the instrument on the outcome. Furthermore, if we also replace outcome Y with intervention D in the respective equations, we get the first-stage effect of the instrument on the intervention. Finally, we can obtain the LATE by dividing the ITT effect by the first-stage effect, similar to the Wald estimand in equation (6.3):

$$\Delta_{D(1)=1,D(0)=0} = \frac{E[E[Y|Z=1,X] - E[Y|Z=0,X]]}{E[E[D|Z=1,X] - E[D|Z=0,X]]}$$

$$= \frac{E[Y \cdot Z/\Pr(Z=1|X) - Y \cdot (1-Z)/(1-\Pr(Z=1|X))]}{E[D \cdot Z/\Pr(Z=1|X) - D \cdot (1-Z)/(1-\Pr(Z=1|X))]}. \quad (6.5)$$

Instrumental Variables

If the characteristics X to be used in the analysis are selected by the analyst (rather than chosen in a data-driven way), the estimation of $\Delta_{D(1)=1,D(0)=0}$ under the assumptions given in expression (6.4) involves estimating both the ITT effect θ and the first stage effect γ using one of the methods introduced in chapter 4, section 4.3. The estimate of the LATE can then be obtained by dividing the ITT estimate by the first stage estimate. Common methods include matching or regression when relying on the LATE representation in the first line of equation (6.5) (see, for instance, Frölich, 2007), inverse probability weighting (IPW) when relying on the second line of equation (6.5) (see, for instance, Donald et al., 2014), or doubly robust (DR) methods that combine regression and IPW (see, for instance, Tan, 2006).

Similar to the discussion in chapter 5, we may identify the important covariates that affect both the instrument and outcome variables from a potentially large set of characteristics X using a data-driven approach. To this end, we can apply causal machine learning (CML) techniques such as double machine learning (DML) to estimate the intention-to-treat and first-stage effects based on the DR expression (equation (4.7)), and then estimate the LATE, as shown in Belloni et al., 2017. Moreover, the analysis of effect to the instrumental variable context heterogeneity and optimal policies discussed in chapter 5, section 5.4 extends to the to the instrumental variable context by relying on doubly robust statistics, as shown in Athey et al., 2019.

6.3 Use Cases in R

To illustrate LATE estimation in R, we consider the effect of participating in a 401(k) pension plan on net financial assets. A 401(k) pension plan is an employer-sponsored retirement savings plan in the US that allows employees to contribute a portion of their pretax income to a retirement account. We first install and load the necessary packages, including the *AER* package for instrument-based estimation and the *LARF* package for access to the *c401k* dataset. We then load the dataset using the *data* command. The *c401k* dataset consists of 9,275 observations of employees, with information on whether they are eligible for a 401(k) pension plan through their employer, which serves as the instrument Z (1 for eligible and 0 for not eligible). Additionally, information on employees' actual participation in such a plan is available, which serves as the intervention, D (1 for participating and 0 for not participating). The outcome variable Y is net family financial assets in thousands of dollars.

We use the *ivreg* command for estimating the LATE—that is, the impact among compliers who are induced to participate in the pension plan when becoming eligible. Similar to the *lm* command discussed in chapter 3, section 3.4, the *ivreg* command requires a regression formula that specifies the outcome and the intervention separated by "~." In our case, the formula is *c401k[,2]~c401k[,3]*, as the outcome and intervention correspond to the second and third columns of the database, respectively. But we also need to provide the instrument for the intervention, which is to be separated from the regression formula by a vertical bar.

So we also include |*c401k[,4]* after the regression formula, as eligibility is stored in the fourth column of our data. We save the output of our instrument-based estimator in an R object named *results*. Finally, we run *summary(results,vcov = vcovHC)* to investigate the impact of 401(k) pension plan participation. The box below provides the R code for the various steps.

```
install.packages("AER", "LARF")              # install packages
library(AER)                                 # load AER package
library(LARF)                                # load LARF package
data(c401k)                                  # load 401(k) pension data
results=ivreg(c401k[,2]~c401k[,3] | c401k[,4])   # run two stage regression
summary(results, vcov = vcovHC)              # show impact
```

Running the code yields the following outp'ut.

```
Coefficients:
            Estimate  Std. Error  t value  Pr(>|t|)
(Intercept)  11.6768    0.7248    16.11    <2e-16 ***
c401k[, 3]   26.7712    2.0236    13.23    <2e-16 ***
___
Signif. codes:  0 '***' 0.001 '**' 0.01 '*' 0.05 '.' 0.1 ' ' 1
```

The number in the first column of the second line gives the impact among compliers. This suggests that participating in a 401(k) pension plan leads to an average increase in net family financial assets of $26,771 (as the outcome is measured in thousands), among employees who are induced to participate because they are eligible. The corresponding *p*-value in the fourth column of the second line is very small ($<2e-16$), implying that given the estimate in our data, we can almost with certainty rule out that the effect is zero in the population of all employees (from which our data were drawn).

However, eligibility for a 401(k) pension plan is not a randomly assigned instrument. Employees with certain characteristics, such as higher-income jobs, could be more likely to be eligible for a pension plan, and simultaneously, a higher income may also influence assets after retirement. This indicates a potential source of confounding, necessitating the creation of comparable employee groups with and without eligibility in terms of characteristics that could impact the outcome before conducting our analysis. To control for observed background characteristics that may jointly affect the instrument and the outcome in a data-driven way, we load the previously considered *grf* package for causal machine learning based on the random forest.

We use the *instrumental forest* command, whose first argument (X) corresponds to the characteristics, which we set to columns 5 to 11 in our data, such that we control for several employee characteristics: *X=c401k[,5:11]*. These characteristics include income, family size, gender, and age. The second, third, and fourth arguments in the *instrumental forest* command correspond to the outcome (Y), the intervention (W), and the instrument (Z), which we set to *c401k[,2]*, *c401k[,3]*, and *c401k[,4]*, respectively. We store the output in an R object named *results*, which we wrap with the *average_treatment_effect* command to investigate the impact. The box below provides the R code for the various steps.

```
library(grf)                                              # load grf package
results=instrumental_forest(X=c401k[,5:11],Y=c401k[,2],W=c401k[,3],Z=c401k[,4])
average_treatment_effect(results)                         # LATE and standard error
```

Running the code yields the following output.

```
    estimate    std.err
   11.908262   1.651121
```

The LATE estimate amounts to 11.908, suggesting that participating in a 401(k) pension plan increases net financial assets by roughly $11,908 (as 1 unit in that variable corresponds to $1,000) among employees induced to participate by eligibility. The output does not provide a p-value, but provides a standard error of our estimate, which measures the variability of our estimate when repeatedly applying the method to a large number of datasets and thus indicates the uncertainty with which we measure our impact. The standard error is rather small relative to the estimated impact, allowing us to claim with high confidence that the effect is positive. Furthermore, we can manually compute the p-value based on the effect estimate and the standard error. As a rule of thumb, the p-value is lower than the 5% significance level if the ratio of the impact and its standard error exceeds 2. This is clearly the case, as $11,908.262/1.651121 = 7.212229$. Therefore, we find strong evidence for a positive effect of participating in a 401(k) pension plan on the total population of complying employees beyond our sample.

6.4 Use Cases in Python

To implement instrument-based impact evaluation in Python, we import the *statsmodels.api* and *linearmodels.iv.model* modules, as well as the *Pandas* library. Then, we load the *c401k* dataset into a Pandas dataframe named *df* and add a constant term to the data using the *sm.add_constant* function to have an intercept. The instrumental variable regression is carried out with the *IV2SLS* command from the *linearmodels* library, specifying the assets outcome (*nettfa*), the pension plan intervention (*p401k*), the constant term (*const*) as the only characteristic to be accounted for, and the instrument (*e401k*), which is eligibility for a 401(k) pension plan. We save the output in an object named *ivreg* and apply the *fit* method to it, running an instrument-based regression to estimate the local average treatment effect (LATE)—that is, the average effect of the 401(k) pension plan among employees induced to participate in the plan by eligibility. We save the results in an object named *LATE* and apply the *summary* method to display the estimated effect of the regression results. The LATE amounts to $26,771 (as the outcome is measured in thousands), which is exactly the same impact as obtained by the R-based estimation in the first use case of chapter 6, section 6.3, and has a *p*-value that is close to zero. The box below provides the Python code for each of the steps.

```
import statsmodels.api as sm                          # load statsmodels library
import linearmodels.iv.model as lm                    # load linearmodels library
import pandas as pd                                   # load pandas library
df = pd.read_csv('data/c401k.csv')                    # load c401k data
df = sm.add_constant(data=df, prepend=False)          # add constant
ivreg = lm.IV2SLS(dependent = df['nettfa'],           # outcome variable
    endog = df['p401k'],                              # intervention
    exog = df['const'],                               # covariates
    instruments = df['e401k'])                        # instrument
LATE = ivreg.fit(cov_type = 'robust')                 # run instrument regression
LATE.summary                                          # results
```

Next, we incorporate observed characteristics into the LATE estimation in a data-driven way, utilizing causal machine learning in Python based on the random forest. We import the *pandas* and *math* libraries, alongside the *LogisticRegressionCV* module and the *ForestDRIV* module for implementing an instrument-based causal forest procedure. Upon loading the *c401k* dataset into a Pandas dataframe named *df*, we select the covariates (X), the outcome

Instrumental Variables

(Y), the intervention (W), and the instrument (Z). Subsequently, we set up the instrument-based forest algorithm using the *ForestDRIV* command with specific parameter choices, such as 2,000 trees in the forest and a minimum of 5 observations in any subset of a tree. The *discrete_treatment* option is set to *True* to accommodate the discrete nature (meaning a limited number of values) of the intervention (limited to values 1 or 0).

The results are stored in an object named *ivforest*, and we proceed to execute the algorithm with the outcome (Y), intervention (W), instrument (Z), and covariates (X) in our data using the *fit* command. The *ivforest.ate(X)* command computes the LATE, saved in an object named *LATE*, while the *ivforest.ate_inference(X)* calculates the standard error and *p*-value, stored in an object named *INF*. Finally, we present the results using the *print* command. The estimated LATE of 10.874 (or $10,874) is comparable to the R-based computation in the second use case of section 6.3. However, the standard error of 10.402 is notably higher, and the *p*-value is rather large (0.296, or 29.6%), indicating increased uncertainty in the LATE estimation. The Python code for each step is outlined in the box below.

```python
import pandas as pd                                           # load pandas library
from sklearn.linear_model import LogisticRegressionCV         # load LogisticRegressionCV
from econml.iv.dr import ForestDRIV                           # load ForestDRIV
import math                                                   # load math library
df = pd.read_csv('data/c401k.csv')                            # load c401k data
X = df.iloc[:, 4:11]                                          # select covariates
Y = df.iloc[:, 1]                                             # select outcome
W = df.iloc[:, 2]                                             # select treatment
Z = df.iloc[:, 3]                                             # select instrument
ivforest = ForestDRIV(n_estimators = 2000,                    # IV forest
    min_samples_leaf = 5,
    max_depth = min(round(math.sqrt(len(X.columns)))+20, len(X.columns)),
    model_t_xw = LogisticRegressionCV(max_iter = 350),
    discrete_treatment = True)                                # discrete intervention
ivforest.fit(Y = Y, T = W, Z = Z, X = X)                      # fit IV forest with data
LATE = ivforest.ate(X)                                        # compute LATE
INF = ivforest.ate_inference(X)                               # compute p-value
print(LATE)                                                   # show LATE
print(INF)                                                    # show p-value
```

7 Regression Discontinuity Designs

7.1 Sharp and Fuzzy Regression Discontinuity Designs

In this chapter, we will discuss another approach to impact evaluation, named regression discontinuity design (RDD), which was first suggested by Thistlethwaite and Campbell (1960). The RDD relies on the behavioral assumption that receiving or not receiving the intervention is determined based on passing versus not passing a certain threshold in a specific index, known as the "running variable." As an example, consider an internet provider who wants to retain customers (i.e., prevent customers from churning to a competitor) by offering them a discount. In this case, the intervention is whether or not the customer receives the discount, while the outcome is their retention. To determine which customers should be targeted for the discount, the provider calculates the churn probability—the likelihood that a customer will switch to another provider—based on various factors such as age, income, and previous internet usage. The churn probability serves as the running variable, and the provider might decide to offer the discount only to customers with a churn probability (i.e., a chance of switching providers) of at least 50%.

Based on this rule, no customers with a probability lower than 50% would receive the discount, while all customers with a probability of 50% or higher would. For example, a customer with a churn probability of 49% would not receive the discount, while a customer with a slightly higher probability of 50% would. In other words, the intervention "jumps" from 0 to 1 if the threshold of 50% in the churn probability, our index or running variable, is reached. This creates a discontinuous change in the likelihood of receiving the intervention at the threshold, which is what gives the regression discontinuity design its name.

How can we use this design, which bases the intervention on passing an index threshold, for the purpose of impact evaluation? The idea of the RDD is to compare the outcomes (e.g., customer retention) of subjects who receive the intervention and those who do not, but who are located close to the index threshold. For example, we could compare the customer retention rates of customers with a churn probability of 50% (who receive the discount) and customers with a churn probability of 49% (who do not receive the discount). Because these two groups are similar in terms of their index value (i.e., churn probability), we compare apples with apples. Therefore, the RDD aims at imitating the experimental context of comparable treatment and control groups. This is based on the assumption that similar index values for subjects just above and below the threshold imply the comparability of those subjects in terms of any background characteristics that affect the outcome (for instance, personality traits that affect the inclination to switch providers). If this assumption is met, we may assess the impact of the intervention "locally" for subjects close to the threshold by comparing the outcomes of subjects just slightly above the threshold (with intervention) to those just slightly below the threshold (without intervention).

There are many potential scenarios in which an intervention is assigned based on a specific index threshold, allowing for the RDD to be used for impact evaluation. For instance, a company might launch a communication campaign aimed at customers whose past expenditures did not surpass a certain threshold, or an educational intervention (e.g., an MBA program) might only admit students who score above a particular threshold on an admission test. However, a crucial condition for the application of the RDD is that the subjects cannot perfectly manipulate or determine which side of the threshold they end up on. For example, if some students just below the admission test threshold could find a way to tweak their results to just pass the threshold, they might differ in important ways from students who accept their original test outcome, such as being more confident or willing to game the system. As a result, the students just above the threshold would no longer be comparable in terms of background characteristics to those just below the threshold, leading to comparing apples to oranges.

Another example is a retailer offering a loyalty card with specific benefits to customers whose past expenditures exceed a certain threshold. If customers are aware of the value of the threshold (say, $600), some may strategically adjust their expenditures to just make it to receive the loyalty card. However, as some customers may be more focused on this optimization than others, the customer groups just above and just below the threshold might differ in terms of outcome-relevant characteristics like purchasing inclination. On the other hand, if the threshold for receiving the loyalty card is unknown to the customers, there is no opportunity for strategic behavior or manipulation, resulting in comparable groups just above and below the threshold suitable for the application of an RDD.

Figure 7.1 illustrates the RDD intuition for the example with the loyalty card as the intervention of interest. The x-axis shows a customer's past expenditures, which is the running variable. Only customers who spent at least $600 in the past receive the loyalty card, indicated by the dashed line that represents the threshold. The y-axis shows a customer's current expenditures, which is the outcome. The dots represent customers, specifically their past and current expenditures. The solid lines represent the average outcomes across the running variable—that is, the average current expenditures of customers at different levels of past expenditures—both below and above the threshold. The RDD exploits the discontinuity in the reception of the loyalty card at the threshold, where customers just above and below the threshold are similar in terms of past expenditures but differ in terms of holding a loyalty

Regression Discontinuity Designs

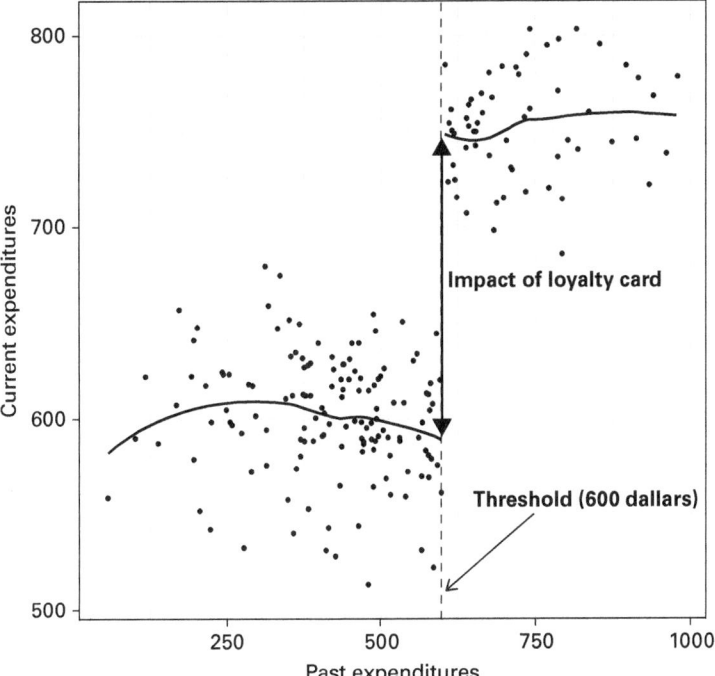

Figure 7.1
Regression discontinuity design

card. The impact of the loyalty card corresponds to the difference in the average outcome (current expenditures) between those just above and just below the threshold, as depicted by the double-edged arrow.

The RDD can also be applied to situations where interventions are assigned based on a threshold in time. Let's consider a retail company that introduces a new pricing strategy at the beginning of the third week in September of a specific year and wants to assess its impact on sales revenue. To evaluate the impact of the pricing strategy, the company compares the sales realized in its stores in the third week of September, the week immediately after the introduction of the pricing intervention, to those of the second week of September, the week just prior to the introduction of the intervention. This analysis utilizes a regression discontinuity in time, as the intervention (implementation of the new pricing strategy) occurs at a specific point in time, allowing for a comparison of outcomes immediately before and after the intervention.

However, it is crucial to ensure that such a before-after comparison is not influenced by differences in any other factors across the two weeks (other than the intervention) that could affect the outcome. For instance, if weather conditions impact shop visits and vary between the second and third week of September, differences in sales between these weeks cannot solely be attributed to the introduction of the pricing strategy but are partly due to different weather conditions across weeks. For similar reasons, it is also important to consider the same (set of) weekdays before and after the introduction, to rule out weekday effects (e.g., more shoppers on Saturdays than on Mondays). Furthermore, one has to ensure that the change in the pricing strategy is not known or expected by customers in the week before the intervention. If customers can anticipate the pricing change and shift their purchases across weeks accordingly, it could contaminate the impact evaluation results.

So far, we have discussed RDD examples that are sharp, meaning that no one below but everyone above the threshold of the index receives the intervention. However, there may be situations where receiving or not receiving the intervention is not solely determined by whether one reaches the threshold of a running variable. This implies that not everyone above the threshold receives the intervention, while some receive it even when being below the threshold. Reconsider the previous example with the test score–dependent educational intervention and assume that all students reaching or passing a minimum test score are invited to an education program (like an MBA), but some students decide to not participate in the program anyway. Likewise, not all customers entitled to a loyalty card according to their past purchases might actually opt to acquire it.

Similar to the discussion of instrumental variables in chapter 6, we have non-compliance in the sense that not all subjects stick to passing or not passing the threshold in terms of receiving or not receiving the intervention. In this case, we may apply a so-called fuzzy (rather than sharp) RDD approach to evaluate the impact on compliers at the threshold—that is, those subjects at the threshold induced to switch the intervention when passing the threshold (from below to above), given that such compliers actually exist. At the same time, passing the threshold must not reduce take-up of the intervention for any subject, which is equivalent to the weak monotonicity condition for instruments discussed in chapter 6. In fact, the fuzzy RDD uses passing the threshold as an instrument for assessing the impact of the intervention.

7.2 Behavioral Assumptions and Methods

To formalize our discussion of the RDD, we define R as the index or running variable (e.g., the churn probability) and r_0 as the threshold value (e.g., 50%). If the intervention is determined solely based on whether the running variable R reaches or exceeds the threshold r_0, then it holds that the intervention $D = 1$ if $R \geq r_0$, while $D = 0$ if $R < r_0$. This is known as a "sharp" RDD, in the sense that all subjects switch their intervention from 0 to 1 exactly at the threshold r_0. Impact evaluation based on the RDD relies on the assumption that any background characteristics other than intervention D that have an influence on outcome Y change only gradually (not abruptly) around the threshold—that is, they are "continuously distributed," in statistical parlance (see, e.g., the discussion in Hahn et al., 2001).

Intuitively, this means that subjects just below and just above the threshold have similar background characteristics. As argued before, this appears plausible if noone can tweak or game the system to influence on which side of the threshold one ends up, such that those just below or just above the threshold are very similar, thus mimicking an experimental setting. As a further condition, there must exist subjects with values in the running variable R that are actually close to the threshold r_0, both below and above. In our example with a threshold value of 50% in the churn probability determining whether someone is targeted by the discount, it must be the case that there actually are customers with churn probabilities around this threshold. This would be, for instance, violated if all churn probabilities were smaller than 40% or larger than 60%.

Under the previously discussed conditions, we can measure a local average treatment effect (ATE) for subjects at the threshold (rather than the total population), which we denote by $\Delta_{r_0} = E[Y(1)|R=r_0] - E[Y(0)|R=r_0]$. Mathematically speaking, we would like to compare the outcomes of subjects with and without intervention whose value in the running variable is situated within a small window of size $\epsilon > 0$ around the threshold (where ϵ is a small, positive value) when letting ϵ getting smaller and smaller—that is, go to zero:

$$\Delta_{r_0} = \lim_{\epsilon \to 0} E[Y|R \in [r_0, r_0 + \epsilon)] - \lim_{\epsilon \to 0} E[Y|R \in [r_0 - \epsilon, r_0)] \quad (7.1)$$

So, ideally, we would like to make the window ϵ arbitrarily close to 0, so that subjects receiving and not receiving the intervention are arbitrarily close in terms of the running variables (and, thus, their background characteristics if manipulation at the threshold can be ruled out). In our previous example with a churn probability of 50% being the threshold, setting $\epsilon = 5\%$ implies that our window includes subjects whose churn probability is within 45% and 55%. In contrast, a smaller ϵ of 1% only includes churn probabilities between 49% and 51%, which is considerably closer to the threshold.

Figure 7.2 visually illustrates the sharp RDD by plotting the average potential outcomes with and without intervention as a function of the running variable R, denoted by $E[Y(1)|R]$ and $E[Y(0)|R]$. In our previous example, the average potential outcomes represent the average customer retention rate with and without providing a discount at specific values of the churn index. The intervention D switches from 0 to 1 at the threshold $r_0 = 50$, indicated by the vertical line in the graph. Therefore, the average potential outcome when receiving the intervention, $E[Y(1)|R]$, is only observed for $R \geq 50$, where $D = 1$, as indicated by the solid line in the graph. In contrast, the potential outcome when receiving the intervention is unknown for subjects $R < 50$ (e.g., a lower churn probability than 50%), where $D = 0$, as indicated by the dashed line. Likewise, the mean potential outcome without intervention, $E[Y(0)|R]$, is only observed for subjects with $R < 50$, where $D = 0$, but not for subjects with $R \geq 50$, where $D = 1$.

Therefore, we cannot compare the outcomes of subjects with $D = 1$ and $D = 0$ for the same value of the running variable R. This stands in stark contrast to chapter 4, where we compared subjects with and without intervention who shared the same values in observed

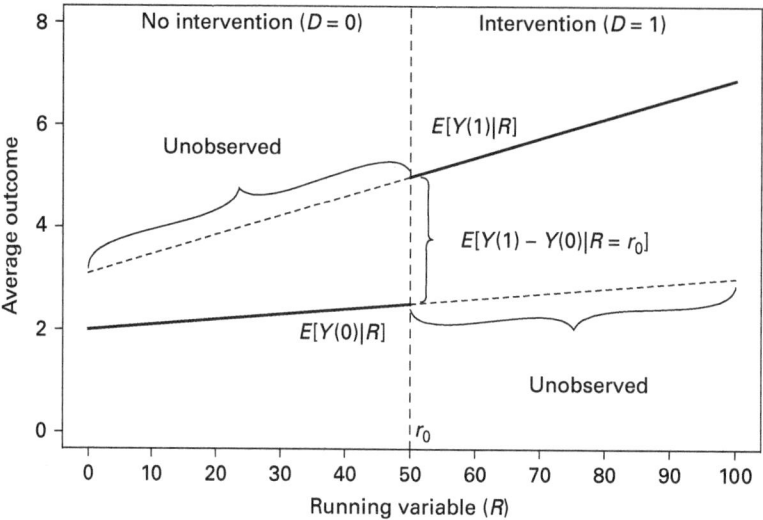

Figure 7.2
Sharp regression discontinuity design

characteristics X. In a sharp RDD, we aim to come close to this approach by assessing the impact at the threshold, Δ_{r_0}, based on comparing the outcomes of subjects just above the threshold (who receive the intervention) and just below the threshold (who do not receive the intervention). If the window ϵ based on which we select observations around the threshold, is sufficiently close to 0, subjects with and without intervention are similar (although not fully the same) in terms of the running variable and, thus, in terms of background characteristics.

In contrast to the sharp RDD, where the intervention is assigned only to those above the threshold, the fuzzy RDD allows for noncompliance, meaning that not all subjects above the threshold may receive the intervention, while even some subjects below the threshold may receive it. Despite this, we can still use the RDD approach to evaluate the impact of the intervention on compliers at the threshold, subjects induced to switch from not receiving the intervention to receiving it as they pass the threshold. However, we must assume that passing the threshold does not decrease the intervention (from 1 to 0) for any individual, as discussed by Dong (2014), and is equivalent to the monotonicity condition for instruments in chapter 6.

To consider the fuzzy (rather than the sharp) RDD, we adjust our notation and define an instrument Z based on passing the threshold. Specifically, $Z = 1$ if $R \geq r_0$, and $Z = 0$ if $R < r_0$. D now corresponds to the actual take-up of the intervention, which may not always align with the incidence of passing the threshold, as previously discussed for the example of passing the test score and subsequent participation in the educational program. Then, we can assess the first-stage effect of the instrument Z on the intervention D at the threshold $R = r_0$, which we denote by γ_{r_0}, when considering a small window around the threshold (analogous to equation (7.1)):

$$\gamma_{r_0} = \lim_{\epsilon \to 0} E[D|R \in [r_0, r_0 + \epsilon)] - \lim_{\epsilon \to 0} E[D|R \in [r_0 - \epsilon, r_0)]. \quad (7.2)$$

Furthermore, in the fuzzy RDD, the impact in equation (7.1) corresponds to the impact of Z on Y at the threshold, denoted by θ_{r_0} (rather than Δ_{r_0} as in the sharp RDD). In chapter 6, we referred to such a causal effect of the instrument on the outcome as the intention-to-treat (ITT) effect.

Analogous to equation (6.3) in chapter 6, we can measure the local average treatment effect (LATE) on compliers at the threshold in the fuzzy RDD by dividing (or scaling) the ITT by the first-stage effect at the threshold, given by

$$\frac{\theta_{r_0}}{\gamma_{r_0}}, \quad (7.3)$$

where θ_{r_0} is the impact of passing the threshold on the outcome Y, and γ_{r_0} is the impact of passing the threshold on the intervention D. As this impact refers to the complier subpopulation at the threshold only, it is an even more localized effect than the LATE considered in chapter 6. To better illustrate the fuzzy RDD, we can use a graphical representation as shown in figure 7.3. This consists of running two sharp RDDs with D and Y as outcomes to measure γ_{r_0} and θ_{r_0}, respectively. We can then scale the latter by the former to obtain the impact of the intervention on the complier subpopulation at the threshold, denoted by $\Delta_{D(1)=1, D(0)=0, R=r_0}$.

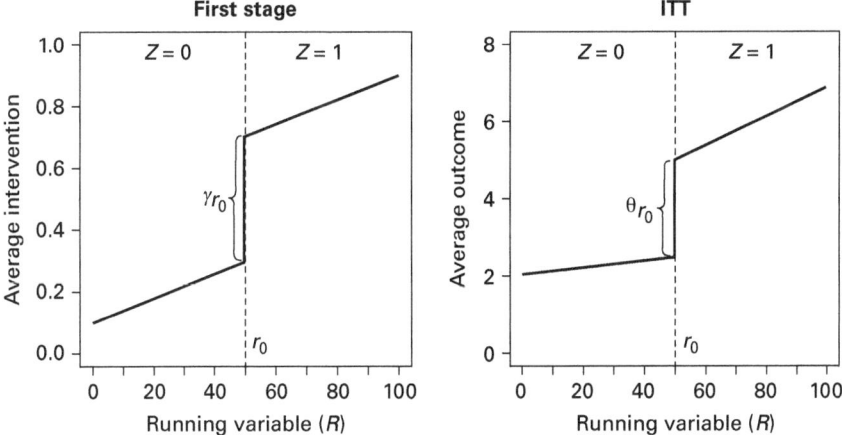

Figure 7.3
The fuzzy regression discontinuity design

In real-world applications of the sharp RDD, impact evaluation mostly involves running a regression (see section 3.2 in chapter 3 for a brief discussion of regression) of the outcome variable Y on the running variable R and the intervention D locally—that is, within a small window ϵ around the threshold. The coefficient on D in the regression then corresponds to the estimated impact at the threshold—that is, the estimate of Δ_{r_0}. Also, for the fuzzy RDD, we may use local regressions for estimating the first-stage effect and the ITT effect, by regressing D on R and Z and Y on R and Z, respectively. To estimate the impact among compliers at the threshold, the coefficient on Z in the ITT regression is divided by the coefficient on Z in the first-stage regression.

A crucial question for such regressions is how large the data window ϵ should be. A smaller window limits the regression to observations close to the threshold, which are more similar in terms of the running variable R (e.g., the churn index) and, thus, background characteristics. This reduces the distinctiveness between observations with $D=1$ and $D=0$ (or bias, to use statistical parlance), which is desirable for obtaining a proper assessment of the impact. In this respect, choosing a data window with $\epsilon = 1\%$ to include only churn probabilities between 49% and 51% appears preferable to using $\epsilon = 5\%$, which includes probabilities between 45% and 55%, for a threshold value of 50%.

A smaller window ϵ, however, has its drawback in that it tends to reduce the number of available subjects within the window, leading to a smaller sample size for impact evaluation. For instance, out of a database of 5,000 customers, only 200 may have a churn probability that is within 5 percentage points of the 50% threshold, and perhaps only 100 may fall within a 1 percentage point range. Basing the estimation of the impact on only 100 rather than 200 observations increases the uncertainty in the estimation, or (to use statistical parlance) its variance. Therefore, choosing the data window or bandwidth ϵ involves a trade-off between bias and variance. A smaller bandwidth decreases estimation bias by making subjects with $D=1$ and $D=0$ more comparable in terms of background characteristics, as they are closer to the threshold. On the other hand, a smaller bandwidth increases variance by relying on fewer observations. Hence, it is desirable to select a window size that optimally trades off or balances the bias and variance to minimize the overall error. There are statistical methods that can calculate the optimal bandwidth for a given database based on these considerations, such as the approaches proposed in Imbens and Kalyanaraman, 2012 and Calonico et al., 2014.

It is worth mentioning that we can partially verify the plausibility of the behavioral assumptions required for RDD-based impact evaluation (somewhat related to the placebo tests discussed in the difference-in-differences (DiD) context of chapter 8, section 8.1). This concerns the previously discussed condition that no subjects must be able to manipulate or tweak the running variable to end up on one side or the other side of the threshold. One way of checking this condition is to examine whether there are similar numbers of subjects situated just below and just above the threshold, as suggested by McCrary (2008). If considerably more subjects are bunched on one side of the threshold than the other, this generally indicates manipulation. Let's reconsider our earlier example of a retailer issuing a loyalty card to customers based on a threshold value, say $600 in past purchases. If customers are aware of this threshold, many may strategically adjust their spending to cross the $600 threshold to secure the loyalty card. In such a scenario, we would observe considerably more customers spending exactly $600 (or slightly more) than customers spending $599 (or slightly less). This bunching would indicate a discrepancy in having comparable groups just above and just below the threshold for receiving the loyalty card.

As a further check, Lee (2008) suggests investigating whether observed characteristics X are similar for subjects just below and just above the threshold. If this is not the case, it suggests that subjects just below and just above the threshold generally differ in characteristics that may also affect the outcome. As a result, we may be comparing apples to oranges rather than apples to apples. For instance, it is possible that customers just above the loyalty card threshold might have different customer characteristics, like income or education, than those just below the threshold. This discrepancy in observed characteristics among subjects just above and just below the threshold might result from certain customer groups (defined in terms of income or education), behaving more strategically with respect to adjusting their expenditures (to just pass the $600 threshold) than other groups.

7.3 Use Cases in R

Let's consider an application of the sharp RDD in R. To do this, we install and load the *rdrobust* and *rddtools* packages using the *install.packages* and *library* commands, respectively. We can then load the *indh* dataset, which is available in the *rddtools* package, using the *data* command. The data were collected to assess the impact of a development aid program in Morocco on interpersonal trust and altruism within communities. More specifically, the intervention is defined in terms of whether a community receives development aid, and we are interested in its impact on prosocial behavior in the community. This is measured based on whether individuals in communities make monetary contributions to (public) goods, which also benefit other community members, in economic games organized by researchers. In this context, the community-specific poverty rate serves as the running variable, and it can theoretically take any number between 0% and 100%. The development aid program is only provided to communities with a poverty rate of at least 30%, such that the threshold value $r_0 = 30\%$.

To assess the impact of the development aid program on prosocial behavior in communities with a poverty rate close to 30%, we apply the *rdrobust* command from the *rdrobust* package in R. By default, this command uses a data-driven method for determining the size of the data window (or bandwidth). The first argument (y) is the outcome variable, which we set to the first column of the *indh* data using the command *indh[,1]*. This variable takes the value of 1 if an individual contributed to public goods and 0 otherwise. The second argument (x) is the running variable, which we set to the second column of the data (*indh[,2]*), containing the poverty rate in percentage terms. The third argument (*c*) is the threshold, which we set to 30. We save the output of the *rdrobust* command in an object named *results*, which we then inspect using the *summary* command to see the estimated impact. The R code for each step is provided in the box below.

```
install.packages("rdrobust", "rddtools")    # install packages
library(rdrobust)                            # load rdrobust library
library(rddtools)                            # load rdrobust library
data(indh)                                   # load indh data
results=rdrobust(y=indh[,1], x=indh[,2], c=30)  # run RDD (threshold: 30)
summary(results)                             # show impact
```

Running the commands gives the following output.

Method	Coef.	Std. Err.	z	P>|z|	[95% C.I.]
Conventional	0.134	0.238	0.561	0.575	[−0.333 , 0.601]
Robust	—	—	0.062	0.951	[−0.664 , 0.707]

The column *Coef.* in the output provides the estimated impact. It indicates that for communities close to the poverty threshold, receiving development aid increases the share of individuals contributing to a public game by 0.134, which corresponds to 13.4 percentage points (as the outcome can only be 1 or 0). The column $P > |z|$ gives the *p*-value computed based on two different methods, *Conventional* or *Robust*, with the latter being the recommended option for the RDD. We can observe that both *p*-values are quite large (0.575 and 0.951), suggesting that when claiming that the true impact in the population is nonzero based on its estimate in our database, we face a substantial type I error probability (i.e., the chance of being wrong with this claim). Therefore, we do not find strong evidence for an effect of the intervention. In a second step, we visualize the effect at the threshold by generating a plot of the outcome against the running variable using the *rdplot* command.

```
rdplot(y=indh[,1], x=indh[,2], c=30)         # plot outcome
```

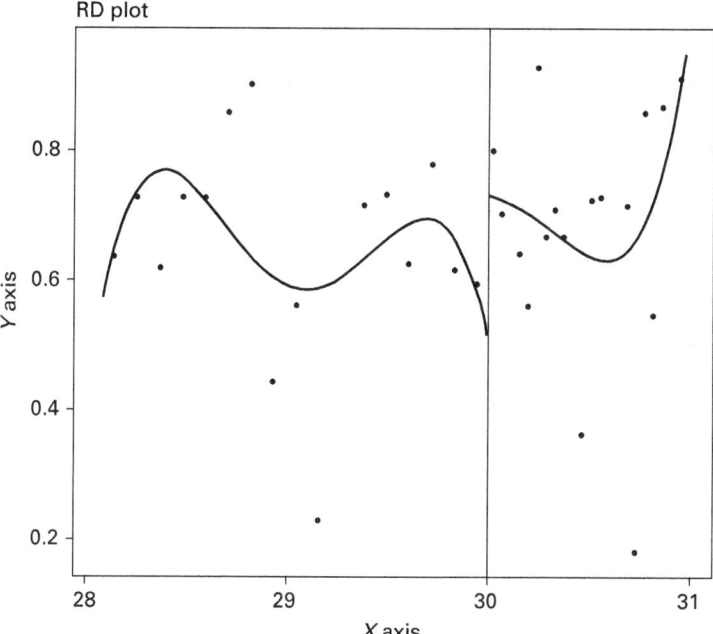

Figure 7.4
Plot of the discontinuity

Running the command produces the plot depicted in figure 7.4. The dots represent the average outcomes within specific ranges (or bins) of values of the running variable, while the red lines correspond to regression functions that approximate the average outcome across different values of the running variable above and below the threshold. We do not observe a distinct change in the level of dots (average outcomes) just above and just below the threshold of 30, which is consistent with the results of our RDD estimation that did not yield strong statistical evidence for an effect at the threshold.

7.4 Use Cases in Python

In this section, we implement the RDD in Python, utilizing the *rdrobust* library. After importing the *pandas* library and the *rdrobust* and *rdplot* modules, we load the *indh* dataset into a Pandas dataframe named *df*. We define the outcome variable (Y), which is the contribution to a public good, and the running variable (X), which is the poverty rate, from the dataset. Then, we execute the RDD analysis using the *rdrobust* function, specifying the outcome (y), the running variable (x), and the threshold (c), which we set to 30. The obtained results are saved in an object named *results*, and we use the *print* command to display the impact at the threshold of the intervention, which is development aid. Additionally, we generate an RDD plot using the *rdplot* function, visualizing the average outcome just above and just below the threshold. We obtain exactly the same estimates as in the R-based analysis presented in section 7.3, and the plot looks like figure 7.4. The Python code for each step is presented in the box below.

```
from rdrobust import rdrobust, rdplot    # load rdrobust library
import pandas as pd                      # load pandas library
df = pd.read_csv('data/indh.csv')        # load indh data
Y = df.iloc[:, 0]                        # outcome variable
X = df.iloc[:, 1]                        # running variable
results = rdrobust(y=Y, x=X, c=30)       # RDD (threshold: 30)
print(results)                           # show impact
rdplot(y=Y, x=X, c=30)                   # plot outcome
```

8 Difference-in-Differences

8.1 Difference-in-Differences and the Impact in the Treatment Group

The difference-in-differences (DiD) approach is another useful method for evaluating the impact of interventions in nonexperimental contexts (see, for instance, Snow, 1855 and Ashenfelter, 1978). This method requires a database that includes outcome measures before and after the introduction of an intervention, as well as a behavioral assumption called common trends. The latter states that for two groups, one of which receives the intervention (treatment group) while the other one does not (control group), the average outcomes in both groups would have experienced the same change over time (i.e., a common trend) if neither group had actually received the intervention. This means that the averages of potential outcomes without intervention, $Y(0)$, in both groups would follow a common trend from a period before the introduction of the intervention (in the treatment group) to a period after its introduction. Based on this assumption, we can compare the before-after change in the outcomes (i.e., the differences before and after the introduction of the intervention) of the treatment and control groups to assess the impact of the intervention.

In fact, the before-after change in the average outcomes of the treatment group reflects not only the impact of the intervention but also the general time trend in outcomes (e.g., a general trend in sales outcomes related to the business cycle). On the other hand, the before-after change in the average outcomes of the control group reflects the general time trend alone since this group does not receive the intervention. To isolate the impact of the intervention, we subtract the before-after change of the control group (which equals the time trend) from the before-after change of the treatment group (which equals the time trend plus the impact). As already mentioned, this approach appropriately measures the impact in the treatment group under the assumption that time trends are the same in (i.e., common to) both groups. In this context, it is important to point out that the common trend assumption does not require the treatment and control groups to be similar in terms of outcomes or any observed characteristics prior to the intervention. The levels of outcomes and background characteristics of the two groups can be vastly different in preintervention periods, like comparing apples and oranges. The common trend assumption, however, requires that the way these apples and oranges change over time in terms of their outcomes, if neither group receives the intervention, is comparable.

To illustrate the DiD approach, let's take the example of a retailer who introduces a new product line in some, but not all, of its stores and is interested in the impact of this intervention on weekly sales per store. Unlike in an experiment, the intervention here is not random, as the stores introducing the new product line are located in specific areas with distinct socioeconomic characteristics (like average income or education) and average sales per store compared to other areas, even prior to the intervention. This makes the treatment and control groups different from each other, like apples and oranges. The DiD approach involves comparing the before-after change in the average weekly sales per store in the areas where the new product line is introduced to the before-after change in the control areas that do not receive the intervention. This gives us the ATET, the average impact in areas that introduced the intervention, when assuming that in the absence of the intervention, weekly sales would have evolved in a similar manner in all areas (for instance, because they are exposed to similar seasonal effects). Suppose sales trends are measured in percentage changes from one week to another. Under the common trend assumption, if sales went up by an average of 3% in the control group of stores, we would have seen the same increase in the treatment group had the product line not been introduced. If sales actually went up by 5% in the treatment group, then subtracting the time trend gives us the average impact of the new product line, which is 5%−3% = 2%.

As another example, let's consider restaurants situated in a specific region. Some of these restaurants implement a discount on beverages through the issuance of e-coupons, while others do not, or they might do so at a later time. This allows for an analysis of the impact of e-coupon provision by comparing the change in beverage sales before and after the implementation of coupons for restaurants that issue them with those that do not. Reimers and Xie (2019) carried out such an analysis for a sample of Texas restaurants. Their findings suggest that e-coupons lead to an increase in demand for alcoholic drinks during the promotion period and, to a lesser extent, even after the promotion ends. Another instance illustrating the application of the DiD approach is presented by Guan et al. (2018), where they assess the impact of food coupons for retail stores by comparing purchasing trends between households exposed to the coupon campaign and those not exposed. The authors uncover a positive effect of coupons on food purchases, particularly in the category of ready-to-eat foods.

Figure 8.1 presents a graphical depiction of the DiD framework. The y-axis shows the average outcome by treatment group and period, while the x-axis displays the time period. The solid lines correspond to the before-after changes in the average outcomes of the treatment and control groups. The dashed line represents the hypothetical evolution of the average outcome in the treatment group if no intervention had been introduced, assuming that the common trend assumption holds. This hypothetical evolution aligns with the outcome change in the control group. The difference between the before-after change in the average outcome of the treatment group and the hypothetical evolution without intervention

Difference-in-Differences

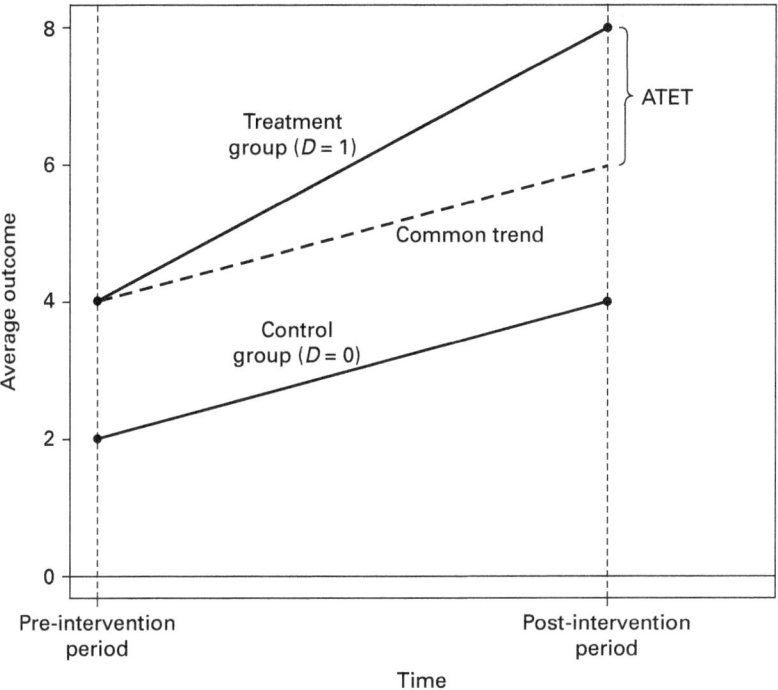

Figure 8.1
Differences-in-differences

represents the average treatment effect on the treated (ATET), depicted by the bracket. This ATET corresponds to the difference in the before-after changes of the treatment and control groups. In this example, the before-after change in the treatment group is 8 − 4 = 4, while that in the control group is 4 − 2 = 2. Therefore, the ATET amounts to 4 − 2 = 2.

It is important to emphasize that if the common trend assumption is not met, the DiD approach does not accurately measure the impact. For example, if the treatment group stores of a fashion retailer are located in a colder region that experienced less summer heat, their sales trends for summer fashion may differ from those of the control group stores. In this case, we cannot assume that both regions are exposed to similar seasonal trends, and thus the DiD approach may not be suitable for impact evaluation. Additionally, it is worth noting that even if the common trend assumption holds, it typically applies to a specific scaling of the outcome variable. For example, if it holds for relative outcome changes over time measured in percent (e.g., sales increase by 3% on average), it typically does not hold for absolute changes measured in specific units (e.g., sales increase by $5000 on average), and vice versa. Therefore, analysts must carefully consider the scale of the outcome variable for which the common trend assumption is most likely satisfied.

8.2 Behavioral Assumptions and Extensions

To formalize and account for the common trend assumption and the observation of outcomes before and after interventions, we introduce a time index T. This time index is set to 0 in the preintervention period when neither group receives the intervention, and it is set to 1 in the postintervention period when the treatment group has introduced the intervention but the control group has not. To differentiate the outcomes between the pre- and postintervention periods, we add the subscript $T = 1$ or $T = 0$. Therefore, Y_0 and Y_1 correspond to the pre- and postintervention outcomes, respectively. We also add these time subscripts to the potential outcomes in the various periods such that $Y_0(1), Y_0(0)$ and $Y_1(1), Y_1(0)$ correspond to the pre- and postintervention potential outcomes, respectively. Using this notation, the common trend assumption can be expressed as

$$E[Y_1(0) - Y_0(0)|D=0] = E[Y_1(0) - Y_0(0)|D=1], \tag{8.1}$$

The equation states that the average difference between the potential outcomes without intervention in the postintervention and preintervention periods in the control group is the same as the corresponding average difference in the treatment group. In other words, both groups have a common trend in the average potential outcomes without intervention.

Besides common trends, another key assumption of the DiD approach is the "no anticipation" assumption. This means that subjects in the treatment group should not anticipate the intervention in a way that affects the preintervention outcomes. For example, if the intervention is a new product line set to be introduced in February 2023 and sales is the outcome, the treatment group should not already change their purchasing behavior in January 2023 (or earlier months) in anticipation of the new product line. Formally, this assumption means that the average treatment effect on the treated (ATET) in the pretreatment period (when $T = 0$) is 0, which can be written as

$$E[Y_0(1) - Y_0(0)|D=1] = 0. \tag{8.2}$$

The causal effect of interest in the DiD approach is the ATET after the implementation of the treatment, which is represented by $\Delta_{D=1} = E[Y_1(1) - Y_1(0)|D=1]$. As already discussed, we can assess the ATET by comparing the differences in average outcomes before and after the intervention across the treatment and control groups. The equation for the ATET can be written as follows:

$$\Delta_{D=1} = E[Y_1(1)|D=1] - E[Y_1(0)|D=1]$$

$$= \underbrace{E[Y_1|D=1] - E[Y_0|D=1]}_{\text{before-after change among treated}} - \underbrace{\{E[Y_1|D=0] - E[Y_0|D=0]\}}_{\text{before-after change among nontreated}}. \tag{8.3}$$

In this equation, the first term represents the before-after change in outcomes among the treatment group, and the second term represents the before-after change in outcomes among the control group.

It is worth noting that if we have the luxury of measuring outcomes in multiple preintervention periods, we can to some extent test the validity of the common trend assumption equation (8.1) in our data. For example, suppose we have information about the sales outcome per store not only in the week before the intervention (e.g., a new product line) is introduced but also two, three, or more weeks prior to the intervention. We can use these preintervention periods to perform placebo tests. To do this, we simply apply the DiD method in a time frame before the intervention by designating an earlier preintervention period (for instance, three weeks before the intervention) as the baseline $T = 0$ and a later, but still preintervention period as "placebo-treatment" period $T = 1$ (say, two weeks prior to the intervention). As no intervention has yet been introduced in either of these periods, the true impact is zero. Thus, the impact obtained from the DiD method in the preintervention periods should also be close to zero. If it is considerably and statistically significantly different from zero, then it suggests a likely violation of the common trend assumption. This is because if sales outcomes in the treatment and control groups have different trends in the preintervention periods, this cannot be attributed to any intervention effect, as the intervention has not yet been implemented. Therefore, the only plausible explanation is that the common trend assumption is not met, implying that sales do not increase or decrease at the same rate in both groups even when no intervention is introduced.

The DiD approach can be extended to scenarios where the intervention is introduced for multiple groups but at different times (see the discussions in Abraham and Sun, 2018; Borusyak and Jaravel, 2018; Callaway and Sant'Anna, 2021; Goodman-Bacon, 2018; and de Chaisemartin and D'Haultfeuille, 2020). For example, a new product line could be rolled out in several areas at different times, such that some stores receive the intervention earlier than others. In this case, we can assess the ATET for multiple groups of stores defined by the period in which the intervention is introduced. The stores that have not yet received the intervention in a particular period serve as the control group for those that have already introduced the intervention. This allows us to evaluate whether and how the effects differ across different areas and time periods. Furthermore, we can investigate whether the impact depends on the time elapsed after the intervention's introduction. For instance, we could evaluate the impact of introducing a new product line on sales one week after the introduction to assess its short-term effect, or 20 weeks after the introduction to see if any longer-term effects on sales persist.

We have already discussed the possibility of the common trend assumption being violated in practice, which is why it is advisable to conduct placebo tests to verify its plausibility. For instance, even in the absence of any intervention, the growth rate of sales in two different regions may diverge due to factors such as income or income growth being higher in one region than the other. Similar to the discussion on instruments in chapter 6, section 6.1, the common trend assumption may be more plausible when the treatment and control groups are made comparable in terms of observed covariates X. For example, comparing only areas with similar economic conditions (such as income) might make it more plausible that the common trend assumption holds across treatment and control groups. Once again, placebo tests may be employed to scrutinize this conjecture. Therefore, we will assume from now on that the DiD assumptions hold only when the treatment and control groups are comparable by controlling for X.

Formally, the measurement of the ATET relies on the following behavioral assumption, as discussed by Lechner (2011):

$$E[Y_1(0) - Y_0(0)|D=0, X] = E[Y_1(0) - Y_0(0)|D=1, X], \qquad (8.4)$$

$$E[Y_0(1) - Y_0(0)|D=1, X] = 0,$$

$$\Pr(D=1, T=1|X, (D,T) \in \{(d,t), (1,1)\}) < 100\% \text{ for all } (d,t) \in \{(1,0), (0,1), (0,0)\}.$$

The first line in expression (8.4) formalizes the conditional common trend assumption, which assumes that for individuals with the same values of observable characteristics X, there are no unobserved factors that jointly affect their chance of receiving the intervention and the trend of the average potential outcome in the absence of the intervention. In other words, the assumption requires that treatment and control groups with the same values in X are comparable with respect to how their potential outcomes would evolve over time in the absence of the intervention. This is a selection-on-observables assumption on intervention D, but with regard to changes in mean potential outcomes over time, rather than the levels of the outcomes as in expression (4.1) in chapter 4.

The second line in expression (8.4) rules out average anticipation effects in the treatment group, conditional on X. This means that among subjects in the treatment group who share the same values in observed covariates X, the intervention D must on average not influence pretreatment outcomes in expectation of the intervention to come. The third line imposes common support: for any value of observed covariates X appearing in the treatment group in the postintervention period ($D=1, T=1$), there must be subjects with such values of X in the remaining three groups— that is the treatment group in the preintervention period ($D=1, T=0$), the control group in the postintervention period ($D=0, T=1$), and the control group in the preintervention period ($D=0, T=0$).

Based on the behavioral assumptions in expression (8.4), we can measure the average treatment effect on the treated (ATET) conditional on X—that is, the average impact of the intervention among subjects in the treatment group with the same values in observed characteristics. We can express this as

$$E[Y_1(1) - Y_1(0)|D=1, X] = E[Y_1|D=1, X] - E[Y_0|D=1, X]$$

$$- \{E[Y_1|D=0, X] - E[Y_0|D=0, X]\}. \qquad (8.5)$$

To obtain the ATET, we can then take the average of the conditional ATET given in equation (8.5) in the treatment group during the posttreatment period. This gives us

$$\Delta_{D=1,T=1} = \tag{8.6}$$

$$E[E[Y_1|D=1,X] - E[Y_0|D=1,X] - \{E[Y_1|D=0,X] - E[Y_0|D=0,X]\}|D=1, T=1].$$

As with the selection-on-observables framework in chapter 4 or the instrument-based approach in chapter 6, we can estimate the ATET through regression, matching, inverse probability weighting (IPW), or doubly robust (DR) estimation (see, for instance, the discussions in Abadie, 2005 and Sant'Anna and Zhao, 2018). We can also use causal machine learning (CML) to control for the most important characteristics among a possibly large number of covariates X in a data-driven way, similar to the methods described in chapter 5. DiD approaches based on double machine learning (DML), as discussed in section 5.2, are, for example, suggested in Chang, 2020 and Zimmert, 2020.

There are practical challenges in measuring the uncertainty or variance of the DiD approach, which is necessary for computing p-values and confidence intervals for the measured impact. This is because the outcome of one observation, such as the sales of a store, is often related to the outcomes of other observations, which complicates variance estimation. For instance, in so-called panel data, the same subjects are observed before and after the intervention, leading to statistical associations of background characteristics within subjects over time. For example, a customer's personality traits in the preintervention period are likely to influence the same customer's traits in later periods, including the postintervention period.

These associations may also occur in so-called repeated cross-sectional data, where different subjects are observed in each period. For instance, customers living in areas receiving or not receiving the intervention may share the same institutional context of the area, leading to statistical associations. For example, if a new product line (as the intervention of interest) is introduced in one country but not in others, all customers living in the same country share the same national legislation (for instance, tax laws or business regulations) and institutions, which may create a statistical relation among those customers. Ignoring these issues can result in an inappropriate measurement of the variance of DiD-based impact evaluation. Therefore, cluster-robust methods for estimating the variance of the ATET should be used in DiD estimation. These methods account for statistical associations by defining clusters of subjects in the data whose unobserved characteristics, such as tax laws, might be related to each other.

8.3 Use Cases in R

To apply DiD estimation in R, we install and load the *DRDID* package using the *install.packages* and *library* commands. Next, we load the *nsw_long* dataset using the *data* command. This dataset provides information on the participation in a US program that offers supported employment to hard-to-employ individuals as a stepping stone to regular, unsubsidized employment. The effectiveness of the program, which is our intervention of interest, was evaluated in the National Supported Work Demonstration (NSW) in the late 1970s. The *nsw_long* data also include information on earnings prior to and after the program in 1975 and 1978, respectively, as well as on additional individual characteristics. We focus on those observations in the dataset without missing information in any of the variables (even though this is generally not ideal for dealing with missing information in data but serves our purpose of illustrating the DiD approach). To this end, we wrap the *nsw_long* data with the *na.omit* command, which drops all lines with "NA" (for not applicable, which indicates missing values) in any variable and save the new dataset in an R object named *dat*.

Next, we estimate the ATET by running the *drdid* command. The first argument, *yname*, corresponds to the outcome, which we set to *re*, a variable that provides the annual earnings in either 1975 or 1978. The second argument, *tname*, corresponds to the time period, indicating whether the outcome is measured prior to or after the intervention, in our case *year* (which is either 1975 or 1978). The third argument in the *drdid* command, named *idname*, corresponds to the personal identifier of the individuals in our sample, in our case *id*. Based on the variables *year* and *id*, we can construct the before-after differences in the outcome *re* for each individual. The fourth argument, *dname*, corresponds to the intervention, in our case the variable *treated*, which is 1 for program participation and 0 for no participation. The fifth and final argument, *data*, corresponds to the dataset that contains the previously mentioned variables, in our case *dat*. The box below provides the R code for each of the steps.

```
install.packages("DRDID")                                              # install package
library(DRDID)                                                         # load wooldridge package
data(nsw_long)                                                         # load nsw_long data
dat=na.omit(nsw_long)                                                  # drop missing values
drdid(yname="re",tname="year",idname="id",dname="treated",data=dat)    #DiD
```

Running the code yields the following output.

```
    ATT    Std. Error   t value   Pr(>|t|)   [95% Conf. Interval]
 846.8884   581.3926    1.4567    0.1452     -292.6412   1986.4179
```

The first parameter, named *ATT*, is what we call the ATET—that is the average impact on those participating in the program. The estimate suggests that the program increased annual earnings in 1978 on average by roughly $847 among participants. The fourth parameter corresponds to the *p*-value, which is 0.1452. This implies that the estimate in our sample is not statistically significant at the 5% significance level, such that we face a nonnegligible type I error probability. Therefore, one might argue that our statistical evidence for a nonzero impact of the program on earnings is not exceptionally strong.

Next, we also include covariates in our analysis to make individuals participating and not participating in the program comparable in their background characteristics X. Thus, we assume that the common trend assumption is met when comparing individuals with and without intervention who are similar in terms of X, as stated in expression (8.4). To achieve this, we modify our previous ATET estimation based on the *drdid* command by specifying the argument *xformla*, which needs to be followed by "=∼" and the variable names of the characteristics, each separated by a "+." We therefore define *xformla=∼educ+nodegree+age+married*, implying that we control for education (*educ,nodegree*), age (*age*), and marital status (*married*). The remaining arguments are the same as before. The box below provides the R code for each of the steps.

```
drdid(yname="re", tname="year", idname="id", dname="treated", data=dat,
xformla=~educ+nodegree+age+married  )                  # DiD with x
```

Running the code yields the following output.

```
       ATT    Std. Error   t value   Pr(>|t|)   [95% Conf. Interval]
   918.4909      597.8166    1.5364     0.1244    -253.2296   2090.2113
```

After including covariates in our analysis, we observed a moderately higher ATET compared to the previous estimation, amounting to an impact of approximately $918. The corresponding *p*-value is 0.1244 (or 12.44%), such that the effect is not statistically significant at conventionally chosen significance levels, such as a 5% level of type I error probability of incorrectly rejecting a zero effect.

8.4 Use Cases in Python

This section illustrates how to implement DiD estimation in Python. We begin by importing the *pandas*, *numpy*, and *doubleml* libraries, along with the *linear_model* module from the *sklearn* library. The dataset, named *nsw_long.csv*, is loaded into a Pandas data frame (*df*), and missing values are removed using the *dropna()* function. Subsequently, we create a binary time variable (*time*) based on the *year* column. If the year is 1975, the time variable is set to 0; otherwise, if the year is 1978, it is set to 1. Additionally, a constant term column (*const*) consisting of ones is added to the dataframe. Next, we utilize the *DoubleMLData* command to generate a DiD-suitable dataset. We specify the earnings outcome (*re*), the intervention (*treated*), where 1 indicates program participation and 0 denotes no participation, the constant term (*const*) as a covariate, and the time variable (*time*). The output is stored in an object named *dml_data*. Following that, we define the statistical models for the outcome (*ml_g*), which is a linear regression, and for the intervention (*ml_m*), which is a logistic regression.

We proceed by applying DiD using the *DoubleMLDIDCS* and *fit()* commands with the *dml_data* and store the results in an object named *did*. Finally, we utilize the *print* command to display the estimated ATET. The obtained result suggests that the program increased annual earnings in 1978 by approximately $848 among participants on average. This result closely aligns with the R-based findings in the previous section. The *p*-value is nearly 0.17 and thus not statistically significant at conventional levels. The Python code for each step is provided in the box below.

```python
import pandas as pd                                  # load pandas library
import numpy as np                                   # load numpy library
import doubleml as dml                               # load doubleml library
from sklearn import linear_model                     # load linear_model
df = pd.read_csv('data/nsw_long.csv')                # load nsw_long data
df = df.dropna()                                     # drop missings
df['time'] = np.where(df['year'] == 1975, 0, 1)      # create time variable
df['const'] = np.ones(len(df))                       # create constant term
dml_data = dml.DoubleMLData(df,                      # create data
    y_col = 're',                                    # define outcome
    d_cols = 'treated',                              # define intervention
    x_cols = 'const',                                # define covariates
    t_col = 'time')                                  # define time
ml_g = linear_model.LinearRegression()               # define outcome model
ml_m = linear_model.LogisticRegression()             # define intervention model
did = dml.DoubleMLDIDCS(dml_data,                    # DiD
    ml_g,                                            # outcome model
    ml_m).fit()                                      # intervention model
print(did)                                           # show results
```

Next, we apply the DiD approach while accounting for covariates to ensure comparability between groups with and without intervention in terms of observed characteristics. The coding steps are akin to the previous Python example, with the only difference being that, when defining the covariates (x), we now also include characteristics (*educ*, *nodegree*, *age*, and *married*) in addition to the constant term: *x = df.loc[:, ['educ', 'nodegree', 'age', 'married']]*. The Python code provided in the box below reflects this modification starting from the point where x is defined. The estimated ATET is approximately $923, which closely aligns with the impact obtained from the corresponding R-based procedure in the second use case in section 8.3. The *p*-value is 14.7%.

```
x = df.loc[:, ['educ', 'nodegree', 'age', 'married']]   # define covariates
dml_data = dml.DoubleMLData(df,                          # create data
    y_col = 're',                                        # define outcome
    d_cols = 'treated',                                  # define intervention
    x_cols = list(x.columns.values),                     # define covariates
    t_col = 'time')                                      # define time
ml_g = linear_model.LinearRegression()                   # define outcome model
ml_m = linear_model.LogisticRegression()                 # define intervention model
did = dml.DoubleMLDIDCS(dml_data,                        # DiD
    ml_g,                                                # outcome model
    ml_m).fit()                                          # intervention model
print(did)                                               # show results
```

9 Synthetic Controls

9.1 Impact Evaluation When a Single Unit Receives the Intervention

In some evaluation scenarios, interventions are not assigned to many or several subjects, resulting in groups of subjects receiving and not receiving the intervention. In case study designs, for example, only one subject (which could be a geographic area such as a specific market) is targeted by the intervention, while all others are not. The synthetic control approach, first proposed by Abadie and Gardeazabal (2003) and Abadie et al. (2010), was specifically developed for such scenarios where only one subject is exposed to the intervention and multiple subjects are in the control group (not being exposed). Similar to the difference-in-differences (DiD) method discussed in chapter 8, the synthetic control method can be used for impact evaluation when outcomes can be measured both prior to and after the introduction of the intervention. However, in synthetic control, the pre- and postintervention outcomes must come from the same subjects who can be followed over time, which is known as panel data. This is in contrast to DiD, which can also be applied if pretreatment and posttreatment outcomes are measured for distinct subjects, which is known as repeated cross-sectional data but is not tailored to the scenario where only one subject receives the intervention.

Let's consider a practical example to better understand the synthetic control method. Imagine a company that introduces a new pricing policy, which is the intervention of interest, in one specific market but not in others. Furthermore, assume that we can observe sales outcomes on a yearly basis for each market. Our goal is to evaluate the impact of the new pricing policy on annual sales in the targeted market—that is, whether annual sales evolve differently in that market due to the introduction of the new pricing policy. To do so, we would like to compare the development of annual sales in the market with intervention, which we can directly observe, to a comparable market without intervention. However, finding such a comparable market may not be straightforward. This is where the synthetic control method comes into play. It creates a comparable market without intervention by combining other markets that are similar enough to the targeted market prior to the introduction of the new pricing policy but did not experience any intervention.

More concisely, the (counterfactual) outcome that the targeted market receiving the intervention would have realized in the absence of intervention is "synthetically" computed. This is done by creating a weighted average of the postintervention sales outcomes of markets in the control groups, which is called the "synthetic control." The weight (or importance) given to any market from the control group for computing this synthetic control depends on how similar it was to the targeted market in terms of sales (and possibly other characteristics) in the preintervention period. The objective is thus to "mix" markets from the control group in an appropriate way such that the generated mix (the synthetic control) closely matches the development of annual sales of the targeted market in the periods prior to the intervention. For impact evaluation, we make the behavioral assumption that the sales outcome of the synthetic control in postintervention periods is representative of what would have happened with the targeted market had the intervention not been introduced. We can then compute the impact on the targeted market by comparing the postintervention outcomes of the targeted market and its synthetic control.

Figure 9.1 provides a graphical illustration of the synthetic control method. The solid line shows the annual sales (on the y-axis) across years (on the x-axis) of the targeted market, in which the new pricing strategy (the intervention) was introduced in 2014, as indicated by the vertical dotted line. The dashed line represents the estimated annual sales of the targeted market without the intervention, based on a synthetic control constructed using data from other similar markets. We can see that the synthetic control is computed so that it closely matches the annual sales of the targeted market prior to the introduction of the intervention. After the introduction of the intervention, any divergence in the sales of the targeted market and its synthetic control are interpreted as the impact of the intervention. We observe that from 2015 onward, the annual sales of the targeted market are higher than those of the synthetic control, suggesting that the new pricing policy has had a positive impact on sales in the targeted market.

9.2 Behavioral Assumptions and Variants

To discuss the synthetic control method more formally, let's consider a dataset with n units (e.g., markets, with n denoting the number of markets), such that a unit's index i is one of $\{1, \ldots, n\}$. We observe each unit over $\mathcal{T}$ time periods (e.g., years, with $\mathcal{T}$ denoting the number of years), such that time index t is one of $1, \ldots, \mathcal{T}$. Accordingly, we denote by Y_{it} the outcome (e.g., sales) of unit i (e.g., sales of the first market if $i = 1$) in period t (e.g., the first year of our data window if $t = 1$). Furthermore, we assume (without loss of generality) that only the last unit $i = n$ in the data is treated in some period $T_0 + 1$, with T_0 denoting the last period prior to treatment, which satisfies $T_0 \geq 1$.

For instance, if $T_0 = 5$, then the fifth year is the last period in which the intervention—for example, a new pricing policy—is not yet introduced in the targeted market, while $T_0 + 1 = 6$ implies that the sixth year of our data window is the first period after the introduction

Synthetic Controls

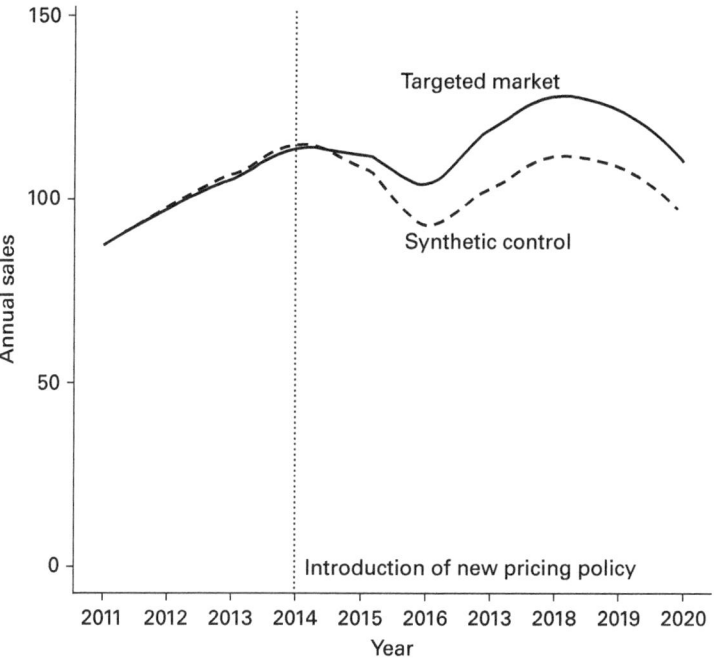

Figure 9.1
Synthetic control method

of the new pricing policy. Therefore, the intervention necessarily takes place in some period after the first period (so that we can measure preintervention outcomes), which implies that $1 < T_0 + 1 \leq T$. In any postintervention period $t \geq T_0 + 1$ (e.g., in the sixth year or later), we may estimate the intervention's impact on the unit receiving the intervention (i.e., for unit $i = n$) by taking the difference between the outcome of that targeted unit and a weighted average of outcomes from the control group. Formally,

$$Y_{nt} - (\hat{\omega}_1 Y_{1t} + \hat{\omega}_2 Y_{2t} + \hat{\omega}_3 Y_{3t} + \cdots + \hat{\omega}_{n-1} Y_{n-1,t}) \tag{9.1}$$

for any postintervention period $t \geq T_0$.

The sum $\hat{\omega}_1 Y_{1t} + \hat{\omega}_2 Y_{2t} + \hat{\omega}_3 Y_{3t} + \cdots + \hat{\omega}_{n-1} Y_{n-1,t}$ represents the synthetic control—that is, the potential outcome of the targeted unit that we would expect in the absence of the intervention. Here, $\hat{\omega}_1, \hat{\omega}_2, \ldots, \hat{\omega}_{n-1}$ are the weights assigned to the units in the control group, which determine the importance given to each unit for computing the synthetic control. The contribution of each unit from the control group to the computation of the synthetic control is determined by the unit's outcome multiplied by its weight. The synthetic control is then computed as the sum of these contributions, which corresponds to a weighted average of outcomes from the control group, where the weights are chosen such that they add up to 100%. For example, the first, fourth, and fifth units in the control group might be assigned weights of 30%, 20%, and 50%, respectively, so that their weights sum up to 100%, while the remaining units in the control group receive a weight (or importance) of zero.

The idea of the synthetic control approach is to choose the weights $\hat{\omega}_1, \hat{\omega}_2, \ldots, \hat{\omega}_{n-1} Y_{n-1,t}$ and, thus, the contributions in a clever way so that the synthetic control corresponds to the potential outcome that the unit targeted by the intervention would have realized without intervention. It is like putting together a puzzle with pieces from other units to create a synthetic version of the targeted unit's potential outcome. To achieve this, the weights are selected such that in the preintervention periods, the synthetic control—that is, the weighted average of preintervention outcomes of units from the control group—closely matches the actually observed outcome for the target unit (which receives the intervention only in later periods). This approach assumes that we can compute the targeted unit's potential postintervention outcome that would have occurred without intervention by applying these weights from the preintervention periods to the control group's outcomes in the postintervention periods.

In other words, making the targeted unit (which receives the intervention) and the control group similar in terms of their preintervention outcomes (Y_{it} for t in preintervention periods $\{1, \ldots, T_0\}$) is presumably sufficient to account (or control) for any factors that may cause differences in the postintervention potential outcomes without intervention between the targeted unit and the control group. Therefore, we assume that similarities in preintervention outcomes ensure a proper assessment of the impact on the targeted unit. In mathematical terms, we choose the weights such that

$$(\hat{\omega}_1 Y_{1t} + \hat{\omega}_2 Y_{2t} + \hat{\omega}_3 Y_{3t} + \cdots + \hat{\omega}_{n-1} Y_{n-1,t}) \approx Y_{nt} \tag{9.2}$$

for all $t = 1, \ldots, T_0$,
where $\approx$ means "very similar" or "approximately the same."

The synthetic control approach is related to the selection-on-observables framework discussed in chapter 4, with preintervention outcomes being used as characteristics to make the targeted unit and the control group comparable, ensuring that we are comparing apples with apples. To better understand this, consider a unit in the control group with very similar preintervention outcomes to the targeted unit, which receives a weight of 100%, while all other units in the control group receive a weight of zero. This is equivalent to pair matching as discussed in section 4.3 when matching on pretreatment outcomes and having only one unit receive the intervention.

Another similarity with the selection-on-observables framework is the reliance on a common support condition that requires the existence of units with and without intervention that are similar in terms of preintervention outcomes. This is known as the convex hull condition, which means that the preintervention outcomes of the targeted unit should not be too extreme compared to the control group. Specifically, they should not be much higher or lower than the highest or lowest outcome among the control group in any preintervention period. In the context of our previous example, this implies that the annual sales of the targeted market prior to the intervention (i.e., the change in pricing policy) should not fall outside the range of annual sales seen in other markets. Additionally and similar to the DiD context in chapter 8, anticipation effects must be ruled out, meaning that the preintervention outcomes of the targeted unit should not be affected by the intervention to follow. Therefore, the annual sales in the targeted market must not already be affected in preintervention periods, such as a reaction to an expected change in the pricing policy.

In addition to considering preintervention outcomes in the construction of synthetic controls, we can also account for characteristics X, so that the generated synthetic control resembles the targeted unit also in these characteristics (in addition to the preintervention outcomes). This is another similarity with the selection-on-observables framework of chapter 4 trying to compare apples with apples. As an alternative, we can also implement a version of the synthetic control method that is more similar to the DiD approach discussed in chapter 8. In this case, the synthetic control is constructed to have a trend over the preintervention periods that is comparable to the preintervention outcome trend of the targeted unit. That is, the change in outcomes across preintervention periods should be similar for the targeted unit and its synthetic control, while the levels in outcomes might actually differ. This is in contrast to the previously discussed version of synthetic controls, which sought to match preintervention levels. When using this DiD approach, we rely on a common trend assumption that is related to the one discussed in chapter 8, rather than a selection-on-observables assumption as discussed in chapter 4. We can even use a data-driven method to choose which version of the synthetic control method (i.e., DiD-based or selection-on-observables-based) performs best in the preintervention periods for mimicking the evolution of the targeted unit's outcome, as implemented in the synthetic DiD method suggested by Arkhangelsky et al. (2019).

The computation of p-values in synthetic control designs does not work the same way as in "conventional" settings with many subjects in both the treatment and control groups. One common approach for approximating p-values is so-called permutation testing (see Fisher, 1935), which estimates "placebo" effects among control group units where the true impact is known to be zero. This is achieved by iteratively considering each unit in the control group to be the "pseudo-targeted" unit (which receives a pseudo-intervention that has no impact) to estimate the placebo effect, while all other control group units are used to construct the synthetic control. This approach permits assessing how "extreme" the impact of the actual intervention on the targeted unit is relative to the placebo effects within the control group.

If the impact of the intervention is in absolute terms (meaning that the effect might be both positive and negative) larger than all or most pseudo-effects, this suggests the existence of a nonzero impact. If, however, many placebo effects are (in absolute terms) larger than the impact of the intervention even though their true value is known to be zero, this implies that the actual impact of the intervention might be zero, as the estimated impact is not particularly distinct from the placebo effects. Therefore, by comparing the estimated impact of the intervention on the targeted unit to the distribution of placebo effects estimated from the control group, we can approximate the p-value. It corresponds to the proportion of placebo effects that are more extreme (i.e., have a larger absolute value) than the estimated impact of the intervention on the targeted unit.

Strictly speaking, permutation testing as described so far is only valid when the intervention is randomly assigned, which is typically not the case in situations where the synthetic control approach is applied. Therefore, p-values derived from permutation testing should be considered only as an approximation. An alternative method for computing p-values is conformal inference, as discussed by Chernozhukov et al. (2021). This method focuses on the placebo effects of the targeted unit receiving the intervention rather than the control group without intervention. The procedure is based on the intuition that if the impact of the intervention in postintervention periods equals zero, then the differences between the preintervention outcomes of the targeted unit and its synthetic control, which represent preintervention placebo effects, must have a distribution comparable to the measured effects in the postintervention periods (the differences between the postintervention outcomes of the targeted unit and its synthetic control). Therefore, permutation is based on reassigning preintervention placebo effects to postintervention periods and postintervention effects to preintervention periods. Subsequently, one can obtain p-values by evaluating how extreme the actual postintervention effects in the original, nonpermuted data are relative to the distribution of permutation-based effects obtained from multiple permuted datasets.

9.3 Use Cases in R

To employ the synthetic control method in R and select the best-performing version (in terms of mimicking the evolution of the targeted unit's outcome in the preintervention periods) using a data-driven method that flexibly incorporates or excludes a DiD approach, we utilize the *synthdid* package, which is accessible on the GitHub software platform. Accessing GitHub requires installation and loading of the *devtools* package, using the *install.packages* and *library* commands. Then, we install the *synthdid* package by running *install_github("synth-inference/synthdid")* and load it using the *library* command. We load the *california_prop99* data using the *data* command, which is a panel dataset containing per capita cigarette consumption information for 39 U.S. states from 1970 to 2000. Our objective is to investigate the effectiveness of a tobacco control program introduced in California in 1989 but not in other states in the US.

The first variable in our dataset, *State*, denotes the unit i, where units correspond to US states. The second variable, *Year*, represents the period T, indicating that the outcome of interest is measured on a yearly basis. The third variable is the outcome Y, which is *PacksPerCapita* and provides information on the smoked cigarette packs per capita for each state in the dataset. The fourth variable is the intervention D, which is *treated*. It indicates the introduction of the Proposition 99 tobacco control program in California in 1989, involving increased cigarette taxes and channeled tax revenues to health and antismoking education budgets, antismoking media campaigns, and local clean indoor-air ordinances. The intervention D equals 1 for observations from California in 1989 or later, and 0 for observations from any other state without the program or California prior to 1989 (the program star).

We then use the *panel.matrices* command to transform the *california_prop99* data into a suitable format for running the synthetic DiD method. The default assumption of this command is that data columns 1 to 4 correspond to i, T, Y, and D, respectively, which is the case for our dataset. We store the transformed data in an object called *dat*. Next, we apply the synthetic DiD method by running *synthdid_estimate(Y=dat$Y, N0=dat$N0, T0=dat$T0)*, where argument Y defines the outcome, $N0$ is the number of nontreated units (38 states), and $T0$ is the number of pretreatment periods (19, from 1970 to 1988). We save the output in an object named *results* and call the latter to investigate the impact. The box below provides the R code for each step.

```
install.packages("devtools")                              # install devtools package
library(devtools)                                          # load devtools package
install_github("synth-inference/synthdid")                 # install synthdid package
library(synthdid)                                          # load synthdid package
data(california_prop99)                                    # load smoking data
dat=panel.matrices(california_prop99)                      # prepare data
results=synthdid_estimate(Y=dat$Y, N0=dat$N0, T0=dat$T0)   # synthetic DiD
results                                                    # show impact
plot(results)                                              # plot impact
```

Running the code yields the following output.

```
synthdid: -15.604 (...)
```

Our estimated impact suggests that the Proposition 99 program reduced per-capita cigarette consumption on average by 15.604 packs per year. This average is computed for the postintervention years from 1989 to 2000. This suggests that the program was effective in reducing smoking; however, we would also like to assess the uncertainty in measuring this impact. To this end, we use the previously mentioned approach of computing placebo effects among control group units by iteratively considering them to be "pseudo-targeted" units to obtain a measure for the so-called standard error, which we already discussed at the end of chapter 6, section 6.3. The standard error characterizes the variability of our synthetic control approach when repeatedly applied to many data points. We obtain the standard error by running *sqrt(vcov(results, method='placebo'))*—that is, by using our previously created *results* and specifying *method='placebo'* to run placebo tests in the *vcov* command, which estimates the variance. Wrapping the variance by *sqrt* yields the standard error; see the R code below.

```
sqrt(vcov(results, method='placebo'))          # show standard error
```

When running the code, we obtain a standard error of roughly 9–10 cigarette packs (it may vary slightly each time we run the command, due to a random component in the placebo tests). Since the size of the standard error is relatively large in comparison to the absolute magnitude of the estimated impact (-15.604 packs per year), this indicates that there is nonnegligible uncertainty in measuring the impact. Finally, we run the *plot* command on the *results* object to visualize the estimated impact of the Proposition 99 program on per capita cigarette consumption across the postintervention periods; see the R code below.

```
plot(results)                                   # plot impact
```

This yields the graph in figure 9.2, which shows the per capita cigarette consumption in California (denoted as "treated") and its estimated synthetic control over time. We observe that the synthetic DiD method is successful in creating a synthetic control that satisfies the common trend assumption (as discussed in chapter 8) in the preintervention periods before 1989. This is because the cigarette consumption of the synthetic control is parallel to that of California over the preintervention periods, indicating that the changes in the level of consumption are comparable (even though the levels are not, but this is not required for the common trend assumption). However, from 1989 onward, we see a divergence of the trends in cigarette consumption, which is arguably due to the implementation of the Proposition 99 program in California. The black arrow in the figure corresponds to the average impact of the program over all postintervention periods (from 1989 to 2000), which we estimated to be -15.604 packs per year.

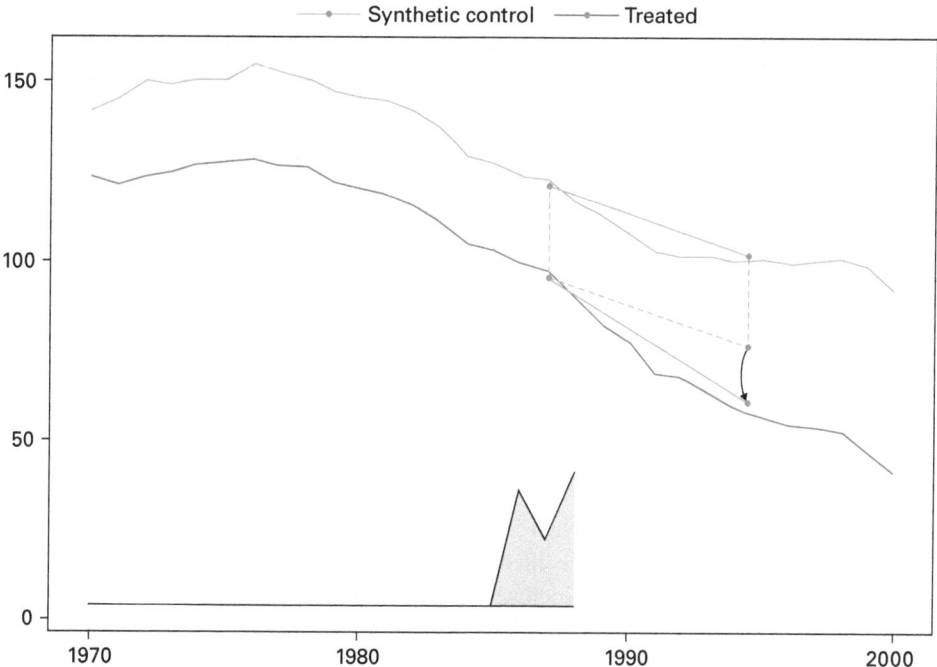

Figure 9.2
Effects based on the synthetic DiD method

9.4 Use Cases in Python

We now consider the synthetic DiD approach in Python. We load the *pandas* and *matplotlib* libraries, as well as the *Synthdid* command and the *california_prop99* dataset from the *synthdid* library. We initiate the synthetic control estimation by applying the *Synthdid* command to the *california_prop99* data, specifying the unit of analysis *i* (*State*), the time period *t* (*Year*), the tobacco control program intervention (*treated*), and the smoking outcome (*PacksPerCapita*). Next, we utilize the *fit()* command to conduct the effect estimation in our data. The *vcov()* command with the *'placebo'* method is then applied to perform placebo tests among the control units for approximating the standard error. The results, including the estimated treatment effect, its standard error, and its p-value, are displayed using the *out.summary().summary2* command.

The estimated effect is equivalent to that obtained from the R-based estimation discussed in the previous section 9.3. This suggests that the Proposition 99 program reduced per-capita cigarette consumption by an average of 15.604 packs per year over the postintervention years from 1989 to 2000. The standard error amounts to 10.52 packs, resulting in a *p*-value of approximately 14%. The Python code for each step is provided in the box below.

```python
import pandas as pd                                    # load pandas library
import matplotlib.pyplot as plt                        # load matplotlib library
from synthdid.synthdid import Synthdid as sdid         # load synthdid library
from synthdid.get_data import california_prop99        # load california data
out = sdid(california_prop99(),                        # synthetic did on data
    unit = 'State',                                    # define unit
    time = 'Year',                                     # define time
    treatment = 'treated',                             # define intervention
    outcome = 'PacksPerCapita')                        # define outcome
out = out.fit().vcov(method = 'placebo')               # placebo se
out.summary().summary2                                 # show results
```

As the concluding step in our synthetic DiD analysis, we utilize the *plot_outcomes()* function to produce a plot visualizing the effects of the program over time. The generated plot is then displayed using *plt.show()*. Notably, the diverging smoking trends in California and their synthetic control after program introduction closely resemble the pattern depicted in figure 9.2 in chapter 9, which was originally generated using R. The Python code for this step is presented in the box below.

```python
out.plot_outcomes()      # plot results
plt.show()               # show the plot
```

10 Conclusion

Impact evaluation is on the rise in firms and organizations like never before. This movement toward evidence-based decision-making has been pioneered by leading tech companies, which place data-based insights at the heart of improving and reshaping business processes. For instance, tech companies employ experiments (or A/B testing) to dissect the effects of interventions in user interfaces, advertising strategies, or algorithmic alterations. This analytical rigor enables tech companies to precisely analyze causal relationships between interventions and user behaviors, to continuously refine their platforms with the aim of enhancing user experience and profitability.

However, impact evaluation extends far beyond the tech domain. In healthcare, pharmaceutical companies rely on these methodologies to assess the efficacy of new drugs or treatment plans. Additionally, impact evaluation plays an important role across diverse sectors and industries for assessing marketing interventions such as advertisement campaigns and discount schemes. Questions regarding cause-and-effect relationships also emerge in various other domains, such as in human resource management when assessing the effect of employee trainings on productivity or accident rates, or in production when evaluating the impact of new technologies on output or production costs.

For answering such questions about causes and effects in firms and organizations, the toolbox of impact evaluation methods has expanded significantly beyond experimental A/B testing. This book has detailed several state-of-the-art methods along with practical examples across its chapters. The applicability of any tool to a specific causal inquiry depends on the institutional context, such as the rule for distributing interventions, and the available data. The growing abundance and quality of data and the availability of increasingly well-designed tools have rendered impact evaluation a strategically ever-more-important approach for decision support and a cornerstone of quantitative business analytics. This is evident in the increasing interest of not only tech companies but also other firms to hire employees with statistical skills for impact evaluation or to invest in training their staff in these methods. Therefore, let's continue exploring and expanding the horizons of impact evaluation in decision-making to make informed choices and foster positive impacts in the dynamic landscape of firms and organizations.

References

Abadie, A. (2003). Semiparametric instrumental variable estimation of treatment response models. *Journal of Econometrics 113*, 231–263.

Abadie, A. (2005). Semiparametric difference-in-differences estimators. *Review of Economic Studies 72*, 1–19.

Abadie, A., Diamond, A., & Hainmueller, J. (2010). Synthetic control methods for comparative case studies: Estimating the effect of California's tobacco control program. *Journal of the American Statistical Association 105*, 493–505.

Abadie, A., & Gardeazabal, J. (2003). The economic costs of conflict: A case study of the Basque country. *American Economic Review 93*, 113–132.

Abadie, A., & Imbens, G. W. (2011). Bias-corrected matching estimators for average treatment effects. *Journal of Business & Economic Statistics 29*, 1–11.

Abraham, S., & Sun, L. (2018). Estimating dynamic treatment effects in event studies with heterogeneous treatment effects. Working paper. Massachusetts Institute of Technology.

AmExpert 2019 Machine Learning Hackathon (AML) (2019). *Predicting coupon redemption*. https://www.kaggle.com/datasets/vasudeva009/predicting-coupon-redemption

Angrist, J., Imbens, G., & Rubin, D. (1996). Identification of causal effects using instrumental variables. *Journal of American Statistical Association 91*, 444–472 (with discussion).

Arkhangelsky, D., Athey, S., Hirshberg, D. A., Imbens, G. W., & Wager, S. (2019). Synthetic difference in differences. Working paper. Stanford University. https://www.nber.org/papers/w25532

Ashenfelter, O. (1978). Estimating the effect of training programms on earnings. *Review of Economics and Statistics 6*, 47–57.

Athey, S., & Imbens, G. (2016). Recursive partitioning for heterogeneous causal effects. *Proceedings of the National Academy of Sciences 113*, 7353–7360.

Athey, S., Tibshirani, J., & Wager, S. (2019). Generalized random forests. *Annals of Statistics 47*, 1148–1178.

Athey, S., & Wager, S. (2021). Policy learning with observational data. *Econometrica 89*, 133–161.

Bawa, K., & Shoemaker, R. W. (1989). Analyzing incremental sales from a direct mail coupon promotion. *Journal of Marketing 53*(3), 66–78.

Belloni, A., Chernozhukov, V., Fernández-Val, I., & Hansen, C. (2017). Program evaluation and causal inference with high-dimensional data. *Econometrica 85*, 233–298.

Borusyak, K., & Jaravel, X. (2018). Revisiting event study designs. Working paper. Harvard University. https://scholar.harvard.edu/files/borusyak/files/borusyak_jaravel_event_studies.pdf

Breiman, L. (1996). Bagging predictors. *Machine Learning 24*(2), 123–140.

Breiman, L. (2001). Random forests. *Machine Learning 45*, 5–32.

Breiman, L., Friedman, J., Olshen, R., & Stone, C. (1984). *Classification and regression trees*. Wadsworth.

Callaway, B., & Sant'Anna, P. H. (2021). Difference-in-differences with multiple time periods. *Journal of Econometrics 225*, 200–230.

Calonico, S., Cattaneo, M. D., & Titiunik, R. (2014). Robust nonparametric confidence intervals for regression-discontinuity designs. *Econometrica 82*, 2295–2326.

Chang, N.-C. (2020). Double/debiased machine learning for difference-in-differences models. *Econometrics Journal 23*, 177–191.

Chernozhukov, V., Chetverikov, D., Demirer, M., Duflo, E., Hansen, C., Newey, W., & Robins, J. (2018). Double/debiased machine learning for treatment and structural parameters. *Econometrics Journal 21*, C1–C68.

Chernozhukov, V., Wüthrich, K., & Zhu, Y. (2021). An exact and robust conformal inference method for counterfactual and synthetic controls. *Journal of the American Statistical Association 116*, 1849–1864.

Cox, D. (1958). *Planning of experiments*. Wiley.

de Chaisemartin, C., & D'Haultfeuille, X. (2020). Two-way fixed effects estimators with heterogeneous treatment effects. *American Economic Review 110*, 2964–2996.

Dehejia, R. H., & Wahba, S. (1999). Causal effects in non-experimental studies: Reevaluating the evaluation of training programmes. *Journal of American Statistical Association 94*, 1053–1062.

Donald, S. G., Hsu, Y.-C., & Lieli, R. P. (2014). Testing the unconfoundedness assumption via inverse probability weighted estimators of (L)ATT. *Journal of Business & Economic Statistics 32*, 395–415.

Dong, Y. (2014). Jumpy or kinky? Regression discontinuity without the discontinuity. Working paper. University of Califronia Irvine. https://mpra.ub.uni-muenchen.de/id/eprint/25427

Dudík, M., Langford, J., & Li, L. (2011). Doubly robust policy evaluation and learning. *Procceedings of the 28th International Conference on Machine Learning*, 1097–1104. ICLM.

Ebbes, P., Papies, D., & van Heerde, H. J. (2017). *Dealing with endogeneity: A nontechnical guide for marketing researchers*, Editors: Christina Homburg, Martin Klarmann, Arnd Vomberg: Handbook of Market Research, pp. 1–37. Springer International Publishing.

Fisher, R. (1935). *The Design of Experiments*. Oliver and Boyd.

Flores, C. A., Flores-Lagunes, A., Gonzalez, A., & Neumann, T. C. (2012). Estimating the effects of length of exposure to instruction in a training program: The case of job corps. *Review of Economics and Statistics 94*, 153–171.

Fong, N. M., Fang, Z., & Luo, X. (2015). Geo-conquesting: Competitive locational targeting of mobile promotions. *Journal of Marketing Research 52*(5), 726–735.

Frölich, M. (2007). Nonparametric iv estimation of local average treatment effects with covariates. *Journal of Econometrics 139*, 35–75.

Gauss, C. F. (1809). *Theoria motus corporum coelestium* (Vol. 1). FA Perthes.

Goodman-Bacon, A. (2018). Difference-in-differences with variation in treatment timing. Working paper. Vanderbilt university. https://ssrn.com/abstract=3246841

Gordon, B., Moakler, R., & Zettelmeyer, F. (2022). Close enough? A large-scale exploration of non-experimental approaches to advertising measurement. *arXiv* 220107055.

Guan, X., Atlas, S., & Vadiveloo, M. (2018). Targeted retail coupons influence category-level food purchases over 2-years. *International Journal of Behavioral Nutrition and Physical Activity 15*(1), 1–10.

Haavelmo, T. (1943). The statistical implications of a system of simultaneous equations. *Econometrica 11*, 1–12.

Hahn, J., Todd, P., & van der Klaauw, W. (2001). Identification and estimation of treatment effects with a regression-discontinuity design. *Econometrica 69*, 201–209.

Hayfield, T., & Racine, J. S. (2008). Nonparametric econometrics: The np package. *Journal of Statistical Software 27*, 1–32.

Heckman, J., Ichimura, H., Smith, J., & Todd, P. (1998). Characterizing selection bias using experimental data. *Econometrica 66*, 1017–1098.

Heckman, J. J., Ichimura, H., & Todd, P. (1998). Matching as an econometric evaluation estimator. *Review of Economic Studies 65*, 261–294.

Hirano, K., & Porter, J. (2009). Asymptotics for statistical treatment rules. *Econometrica 77*, 1683–1701.

Ho, T. K. (1995). Random decision forests. In *Proceedings of 3rd international conference on document analysis and recognition* (Vol. 1, pp. 278–282). IEEE. Institute of Electrical and Electronics Engineers

References

Hoerl, A. E., & Kennard, R. W. (1970). Ridge regression: Biased estimation for nonorthogonal problems. *Technometrics 12*, 55–67.

Holland, P. (1986). Statistics and causal inference. *Journal of American Statistical Association 81*, 945–970.

Horvitz, D., & Thompson, D. (1952). A generalization of sampling without replacement from a finite population. *Journal of American Statistical Association 47*, 663–685.

Huber, M., Meier, J., & Wallimann, H. (2022). Business analytics meets artificial intelligence: Assessing the demand effects of discounts on Swiss train tickets. *Transportation Research Part B: Methodological 163*, 22–39.

Imai, K., & Ratkovic, M. (2013). Estimating treatment effect heterogeneity in randomized program evaluation. *Annals of Applied Statistics 7*, 443–470.

Imbens, G., & Kalyanaraman, K. (2012). Optimal bandwidth choice for the regression discontinuity estimator. *Review of Economic Studies 79*, 933–959.

Imbens, G. W., & Angrist, J. (1994). Identification and estimation of local average treatment effects. *Econometrica 62*, 467–475.

Kassambara, A. (2019). datarium: Data bank for statistical analysis and visualization. R package. https://cran.r-project.org/web/packages/datarium/datarium.pdf

Kennedy, E. H., Ma, Z., McHugh, M. D., & Small, D. S. (2017). Non-parametric methods for doubly robust estimation of continuous treatment effects. *Journal of the Royal Statistical Society Series B 79*, 1229–1245.

Khan, S., & Tamer, E. (2010). Irregular identification, support conditions, and inverse weight estimation. *Econometrica 78*, 2021–2042.

Kitagawa, T., & Tetenov, A. (2018). Who should be treated? empirical welfare maximization methods for treatment choice. *Econometrica 86*, 591–616.

Langen, H., & Huber, M. (2023). How causal machine learning can leverage marketing strategies: Assessing and improving the performance of a coupon campaign. *PLOS ONE 18*(1), e0278937.

Lechner, M. (2011). The estimation of causal effects by difference-in-difference methods. *Foundations and Trends in Econometrics 4*, 165–224.

Lechner, M., Miquel, R., & Wunsch, C. (2011). Long-run effects of public sector sponsored training in West Germany. *Journal of the European Economic Association 9*, 742–784.

Lee, D. (2008). Randomized experiments from non-random selection in U.S. house elections. *Journal of Econometrics 142*, 675–697.

Manski, C. F. (2004). Statistical treatment rules for heterogeneous populations. *Econometrica 72*, 1221–1246.

McCrary, J. (2008). Manipulation of the running variable in the regression discontinuity design: A density test. *Journal of Econometrics 142*, 698–714.

McCulloch, W., & Pitts, W. (1943). A logical calculus of ideas immanent in nervous activity. *Bulletin of Mathematical Biophysics 5*(4), 115–133.

Morgan, J. N., & Sonquist, J. A. (1963). Problems in the analysis of survey data, and a proposal. *Journal of the American Statistical Association 58*, 415–434.

Nadaraya, E. A. (1964). On estimating regression. *Theory of Probability & Its Applications 9*, 141–142.

Neyman, J. (1923). On the application of probability theory to agricultural experiments. Essay on principles. *Statistical Science Reprint, 5*, 463–480.

Neyman, J. (1959). *Optimal asymptotic tests of composite statistical hypotheses*, pp. 416–444. Wiley.

Pearl, J. (2000). *Causality: Models, reasoning, and inference*. Cambridge University Press.

Reimers, I., & Xie, C. (2019). Do coupons expand or cannibalize revenue? Evidence from an e-market. *Management Science 65*(1), 286–300.

Ripley, B. D. (1996). *Pattern recognition and neural networks*. Cambridge University Press.

Robins, J. M., & Rotnitzky, A. (1995). Semiparametric efficiency in multivariate regression models with missing data. *Journal of the American Statistical Association 90*, 122–129.

Robins, J. M., Rotnitzky, A., & Zhao, L. (1994). Estimation of regression coefficients when some regressors are not always observed. *Journal of the American Statistical Association 90*, 846–866.

Robins, J. M., Rotnitzky, A., & Zhao, L. (1995). Analysis of semiparametric regression models for repeated outcomes in the presence of missing data. *Journal of the American Statistical Association 90*, 106–121.

Rosenbaum, P. R., & Rubin, D. B. (1983). The central role of the propensity score in observational studies for causal effects. *Biometrika 70*, 41–55.

Rosenbaum, P. R., & Rubin, D. B. (1985). Constructing a control group using multivariate matched sampling methods that incorporate the propensity score. *American Statistician 39*, 33–38.

Rubin, D. (1980). Comment on 'randomization analysis of experimental data: The Fisher randomization test' by D. Basu. *Journal of the American Statistical Association 75*, 591–593.

Rubin, D. B. (1974). Estimating causal effects of treatments in randomized and nonrandomized studies. *Journal of Educational Psychology 66*, 688–701.

Rubin, D. B. (1979). Using multivariate matched sampling and regression adjustment to control bias in observational studies. *Journal of the American Statistical Association 74*, 318–328.

Sant'Anna, P. H. C., & Zhao, J. B. (2018). Doubly robust difference-in-differences estimators. Working paper. Vanderbilt University. https://papers.ssrn.com/sol3/papers.cfm?abstract_id=3293315

Semenova, V., & Chernozhukov, V. (2021). Debiased machine learning of conditional average treatment effects and other causal functions. *Econometrics Journal 24*, 264–289.

Snow, J. (1855). *On the mode of communication of cholera*. John Churchill, New Burlington Street.

Tan, Z. (2006). Regression and weighting methods for causal inference using instrumental variables. *Journal of the American Statistical Association 101*, 1607–1618.

Thistlethwaite, D., & Campbell, D. (1960). Regression-discontinuity analysis: An alternative to the ex post facto experiment. *Journal of Educational Psychology 51*, 309–317.

Tibshirani, R. (1996). Regresson shrinkage and selection via the lasso. *Journal of the Royal Statistical Society 58*, 267–288.

van der Laan, M. J., Polley, E. C., & Hubbard, A. E. (2007). Super learner *Statistical Applications in Genetics and Molecular Biology 6*.

Wager, S., & Athey, S. (2018). Estimation and inference of heterogeneous treatment effects using random forests. *Journal of the American Statistical Association 113*, 1228–1242.

Wald, A. (1940). The fitting of straight lines if both variables are subject to error. *Annals of Mathematical Statistics 11*, 284–300.

Watson, G. S. (1964). Smooth regression analysis. *Sankhya: The Indian Journal of Statistics, Series A (1961-2002) 26*, 359–372.

Wright, P. G. (1928). *The tariff on animal and vegetable oils*. Macmillan.

Xie, Y., Chen, N., & Shi, X. (2018). False discovery rate controlled heterogeneous treatment effect detection for online controlled experiments. In *Proceedings of the 24th ACM SIGKDD International Conference on Knowledge Discovery & Data Mining*, pp. 876–885. https://dl.acm.org/doi/abs/10.1145/3219819.3219860

Zhou, Z.-H. (2012). *Ensemble methods: foundations and algorithms*. Chapman & Hall/CRC.

Zimmert, M. (2020). Efficient difference-in-differences estimation with high-dimensional common trend confounding. *arXiv* 1809.01643.

Index

*** Page numbers followed by an *f* denote a figure.

A/B testing, 3, 21*f*
  analysis of, methods, 22–26
  behavioral assumptions, 22–26
  comparing apples to apples, 19–21
  leaflet campaign use case, 29–31
  limited scope of, 37
  multiple interventions in, 26–29, 27*f*
  newspaper advertising use case, 31–33, 32*f*, 33*f*
  notation for, 8–11, 22–23
  Python, use cases in, 33–35
  R software, use cases in, 29–33
  sampling bias in, 37
  short-term effects vs. long-term impacts, 37
  uses of, 19–21
  waste production awareness use case, 34–35
Accuracy, 67
Anticipation effects, 127
Artificial intelligence (AI), 2. *See also* Causal machine learning; Machine learning algorithms
Assumptions. *See also* Behavioral assumptions; Selection-on-observables assumption
  common support assumption, 41–42, 126
  common trend, 111–116, 113*f*, 119, 127
  instrument validity assumption, 89, 90
  monotonicity assumption, 88, 90, 104
  no anticipation assumption, 114
  stable unit treatment value assumption, 10
  weak monotonicity assumption, 88
ATE. *See* Average treatment effect
ATENT (average treatment effect on the nontreated), 12
ATET. *See* Average treatment effect on the treated
ATT. *See* Average treatment effect on the treated
Average causal effect (Δ), 11, 23
Averages, weighted, 124–126
Average treatment effect (ATE), 14, 16
  coupon campaign use case, 52, 54, 55
  heterogeneous effects and, 69, 70*f*
  leaflet campaign use case, 30–31
  pair matching and, 43
  Python, 55
  regression discontinuity designs, 103
  regression models and, 46
  R software, 52, 54
  from sample vs. population, 22–26
  in selection-on-observables framework, 42
Average treatment effect on the nontreated (ATENT), 12
Average treatment effect on the treated (ATET or ATT), 11
  in differences-in-differences approach, 112, 113, 114, 115, 116, 119
  pair matching and, 43
  regression models and, 46
  in selection-on-observables framework, 42

Background characteristics (U), 3, 12–16, 16*f*
  in A/B testing, 22–23
  CATEs and, 76
  common trend assumption and, 111–112, 119
  panel data and, 117
  propensity score matching, 45
  random assignment, 19, 20*f*, 22
  random forest and, 95
  regression discontinuity designs and, 100, 102–104, 106
  treatment groups, 12–15, 16*f*
Before-after change in outcomes, 111–113, 115
Behavioral assumptions, 10, 17
  differences-in-differences (DiD), 111–112, 114–117
  in experiments, 22–26
  instrumental variables and, 89–93
  in observational data, 41–42
  in regression discontinuity designs, 99, 102–107
  selection-on-observables assumption and, 41–42
  synthetic controls and, 124–128
  treatment groups and, 41–42

CACE (complier average causal effect), 89
Caliper matching, 44

CATEs (conditional average treatment effects), 72, 75–78, 76*f*, 81, 84
Causal effects, 39–40
Causal forests, 71, 75, 81. *See also* Random forests
Causal inference, fundamental problem of, 7–8, 9
Causal machine learning (CML), 4
 characteristics, most important, 61, 63, 73, 78, 83
 coupon campaign use case, 61–62
 decision trees, 64–67, 66*f*
 in differences-in-differences (DiD), 117
 doubly robust estimation and, 63–64
 effect heterogeneity analysis, 69–74, 70*f*
 elements of, 63–64
 ensemble method, 68
 impacts, detection of differences in, 4
 Lasso, 67–68
 machine learning algorithms, 64–69
 motivating, 59–63
 multiple tasks on subsamples, performing, 64, 65
 neural networks, 68, 68*f*
 optimal policy learning, 62–63, 69–74
 overview of, 60–61
 propensity scores and, 63
 Python, use cases in, 80–85
 ridge regression, 67–68
 R software, use cases in, 74–80
 selection-on-observables assumption and, 60–61
 stepwise regression, 67
 subpopulations, differing impacts, 61, 62*f*
 targeting strategy, optimization of, 62–63
 train ticket discounts use case, 61
Causal trees, 70–72, 71*f*
Ceteris paribus condition, 14
Characteristics, consumer
 causal machine learning and, 60–61
 most important, 61, 63, 67
 wealth of, 59–60
Characteristics, observed, 37–41. *See also* Covariates
Characteristics, unobserved, 38, 39
Coefficients, 23–24, 24*f*
Common support assumption, 41–42, 126
Common trend assumption
 in differences-in-differences approach, 111–116, 113*f*, 127
 plausibility of, 115–116
 R software, use cases in, 119
 validity of, 115
Community development aid use case
 Python, use cases in, 109–110
 regression discontinuity designs, 107–109, 109*f*
Compliance, imperfect, 87
Complier average causal effect (CACE), 89
Complier effects, 87–89
Conditional average treatment effects (CATEs), 72, 75–78, 76*f*, 81, 84
Confidence intervals, 32, 33
 causal machine learning and, 62

 causal trees and, 70
 definition, 25–26
 differences-in-differences and, 117
 differences-in-differences approach and, 117
 linear regression, 25–26
Conformal inference, 128
Consumer characteristics
 causal machine learning and, 60–61
 most important, 61, 63
 wealth of, 59–60
Continuously distributed interventions, 26–27, 102
Control groups
 background characteristics, 12–15, 16*f*
 behavioral assumptions and, 41–42
 covariates and, 37–38, 38*f*
 random assignment, 19, 20*f*
Convex hull condition, 126–127
Coupon campaign use case
 average treatment effect, 52, 54, 55
 causal machine learning and, 61–62
 differences-in-differences (DiD), 112
 doubly robust estimation, 53, 56–57
 effect heterogeneity analysis, 82, 84
 inverse probability weighting, 52–53, 55–56
 optimal policy learning, 78, 84
 pair matching, 51–52, 55
 Python, 54–57, 80–85, 85*f*
 R software, 50–54, 75–79
Covariates, 3, 37–39, 38*f*, 40
 behavioral assumptions and, 41–42
 in differences-in-differences (DiD), 119, 121
 in instrumental variable approach, 91–92, 92*f*
 observational data, 37–39, 38*f*, 40
 in propensity score matching, 45
 treatment groups and, 37–38, 38*f*
Cross-fitting, 64, 65, 67
Cross-validation, 67–68
Customer churn, 12–13, 99
Customer retention rates, 99
Customer segmentation, 73–74, 79–80, 84–85

Data-splitting, 64–65, 70–71
Data subsets, 64–65
Data window, size of, 106
Decision trees, 64–67, 66*f*, 70
Deep learning, 68
Differences-in-differences (DiD) approach, 5, 113*f*
 average treatment effect on the treated, 112, 113, 114, 115, 116, 119
 behavioral assumptions and, 111–112, 114–117
 causal machine learning in, 117
 common trend assumption, 111–112
 coupon campaign use study, 112
 covariates in, 119, 121
 double machine learning and, 117
 employment program use case, 118–119
 Python, use cases in, 119–121

Index

R software, use cases in, 117–119
synthetic controls and, 123, 127, 131*f*, 132
treatment group, impact in, 111–113, 113*f*
variance, measuring, 117
Double machine learning (DML), 63–64, 93
differences-in-differences and, 117
Python, use cases in, 80–85, 85*f*
R software, use cases in, 74–79, 76*f*
Doubly robust (DR) estimation, 48–49
causal machine learning and, 63–64
coupon campaign use case, 53, 56–57
Python, 56–57
R software, 53

E-commerce websites, A/B testing and, 19–20
Ecosystem Europe, 29
Effect heterogeneity analysis, 69–74, 70*f*
causal (random) forests, 71
causal trees, 70–72, 71*f*
coupon campaign use case, 82, 84
individualized effects and, 72–73
lasso regression, 71
policy trees, 73–74, 74*f*
train ticket discounts use case, 72–73
Employee training programs, 8, 9, 40, 42, 49
Employment program use case, 118–119
Ensemble method, 68
Errors, 63–64. *See also* Standard errors
Exclusion restriction, 88, 90
Expectations (E), 11
Experiments (A/B testing), 3, 21*f*
analysis of, methods, 22–26
behavioral assumptions, 22–26
comparing apples to apples, 19–21
leaflet campaign use case, 29–31
limited scope of, 37
multiple interventions in, 26–29, 27*f*
newspaper advertising use case, 31–33, 32*f*, 33*f*
notation for, 8–11, 22–23
Python, use cases in, 33–35
R software, use cases in, 29–33
sampling bias in, 37
short-term effects vs. long-term impacts, 37
uses of, 19–21
waste production awareness use case, 34–35

Financial consultation use case, 87–88, 88*f*
First-stage effects, 91, 92, 93
Forecasting, 1–2
Fuzzy regression discontinuity designs, 102, 104–105, 105*f*, 106

General time trend, 111
GitHub, 128

"Hat" symbol, 22–23
Heterogeneity analysis, 61, 62*f*

Heterogeneous effects, 69, 70*f*
Heterogeneous impact, 28–29, 28*f*
Homogeneous impact, 27, 27*f*, 28

Identifying assumptions. *See* Behavioral assumptions
Impact evaluation
characterizing impact, 8–12, 9*f*, 10*f*
data-based, 2
fundamental problem of, 7–8
methods for, 42–49
overview of, 2
selection bias, 12–17, 14*f*, 15*f*, 16*f*
single unit receives intervention, 123–124
wide use and importance of, 133
Imperfect compliance, 87
Independence condition, 22, 89
Index threshold, 99–100, 104–105. *See also* Running variables
Instrumental variable approach, 4, 88–93, 90*f*, 92*f*
Instrumental variables
behavioral assumptions and methods, 89–93
instruments and complier effects, 87–89
Python, use cases in, 96–97
R software, use cases in, 93–95
Instrument propensity scores, 92
Instruments, 87–89, 88*f*
Instrument validity assumption, 89, 90
Intention-to-treat (ITT) effect, 92–93, 105
Interference effects, 10
Intervals, 25–26
Interventions (D), 8–10, 9*f*, 123–124
Inverse probability weighting (IPW), 46–49, 47*f*
coupon campaign use case, 52–53, 55–56
errors, sensitivity to, 63–64
Python, 55–56
regression models and, 48
R software, 52–53

Kernel regression, 29, 31–33, 32*f*, 33*f*

Lasso, 67–68
Lasso regression, 71, 72, 75
LATE. *See* Local average treatment effect
Leaflet campaign use case, 29–31
Linear regression, 23–24, 24*f*
confidence intervals, 25–26
homogeneous impact and, 28
leaflet campaign use case, 30–31
p-value, 25
variance, 25–26
Local average treatment effect (LATE), 89, 90–91, 92–93
Python, use cases in, 96–97
regression discontinuity designs, 103, 105
R software, use cases in, 93–95
Logit regression, 45

Loyalty card use cases, 3, 12, 16–17
  instrumental variable approach, 89
  regression discontinuity designs, 100–101, 101*f*, 107
  selection-on-observables assumption and, 38

Machine learning (ML) algorithms, 3–4, 64
  decision trees, 65–67, 66*f*, 70
  ensemble method, 68
  Lasso, 67–68
  neural networks, 68, 68*f*
  predictive, 69
  ridge regression, 67–68
  stepwise regression, 67
  uses of, 1–2
Mahalanobis distance, 43
Marketing campaigns, evaluation of, 7, 11–12
Matching
  caveats in, 44
  errors, sensitivity to, 63–64
  for impact evaluation, 42–44, 43*f*
  one-to-many (1:M), 43, 44*f*
  pair matching, 42–43, 43*f*, 44*f*
  propensity score matching, 44–45, 45*f*
  radius, or caliper, matching, 44
Moderation analysis, 61
Monotonicity assumption, 88, 90, 104
Morocco, 107–109
Multiple interventions, in A/B testing, 26–29, 27*f*
Multiple tasks on subsamples, performing, 64, 65

National Supported Work (NSW) Demonstration, 118
Neural networks (NN), 68, 68*f*
New product lines, differences-in-differences and, 112, 114, 115, 117
Newspaper advertising use case, 31–33, 32*f*, 33*f*
No anticipation assumption, 114
Nodes, 68
Noncompliance, 104
Nonparametric regression, 29, 46
Notation
  for A/B testing, 8–11, 22–23
  for coefficients, 23
  "hat" symbol, 22–23
  for interventions (D), 8–10, 9*f*
  for outcomes, 8–10, 9*f*
  for variables, 8–11, 9*f*

Observational data
  behavioral assumptions, 41–42
  characteristics, making groups comparable in, 37–41
  common support assumption, 41–42
  covariates, 37–39, 38*f*, 40
  impact evaluation, methods for, 42–49
  Python, use cases in, 54–57
  R software, use cases in, 49–54
  selection-on-observables assumption, 38–40, 39*f*, 41*f*
  weighting by propensity scores, 46–48, 47*f*
Observed characteristics. *See* Characteristics, observed
One-to-many (1:M) matching, 43, 44*f*
Optimal policy learning, 69–74
  causal machine learning and, 62–63
  coupon campaign use case, 78, 84
  individualized effects and, 73
Optimal targeting strategies, 62–63, 73–74
Outcomes (Y)
  before-after change in, 111–113, 115
  cause and effects, determining, 7–8
  notation for, 8–10, 9*f*
Overfitting, 64

Pair matching, 44*f*
  coupon campaign use case, 51–52, 55
  for impact evaluation, 42–43, 43*f*
  Python, 55
  R software, 51–52
Panel data, 117
Pension plan participation use case
  Python, 96–97
  R software, 93–95
Permutation testing, 127–128
Placebo effects, 127–128, 129–130
Placebo tests, 115
Plausibility, of common trend assumption, 115
Policy trees
  effect heterogeneity analysis, 73–74, 74*f*
  Python, use cases in, 84–85, 85*f*
  R software, use cases in, 79–80, 80*f*
Populations, 11, 22–26
Prediction, 1–2
  decision trees and, 65–67, 66*f*
  machine learning algorithms, 69
Predictive machine learning, 69
Preintervention outcomes, 125–127
Pricing strategies
  evaluation of, 7
  regression discontinuity designs, 101–102
  selection-on-observables assumption and, 38–40, 39*f*
  synthetic controls, 123–126
Probability scores, 45
Probit regression, 45
Propensity score matching, 44–45, 45*f*
Propensity scores
  causal machine learning and, 63
  extreme, 48
  in instrumental variable approach, 92
  weighting observations by, 46–48, 47*f*
Proposition 99, 129, 131
Pseudo-targeted units, 127, 130
p-values, 25
  coupon campaign use case, 51, 53, 77, 80, 83

Index

differences-in-differences and, 117, 119
leaflet campaign use case, 31
linear regression, 25
newspaper advertising use case, 33
pension plan participation use study, 95
synthetic controls and, 127–128
Python, use cases in, 2, 33–35
   A/B testing, 33–35
   average treatment effect, 55
   causal machine learning, 80–85
   community development aid, 109–110
   coupon campaign use study, 54–57, 80–85, 85f
   differences-in-differences, 119–121
   double machine learning, 80–85, 85f
   doubly robust estimation, 56–57
   instrumental variables, 96–97
   inverse probability weighting, 55–56
   local average treatment effect and, 96–97
   observational data, 54–57
   pair matching, 55
   pension plan participation use case, 96–97
   policy trees, 84–85, 85f
   regression discontinuity designs, 109–110
   synthetic controls, 131–132
   tobacco control program use case, 131–132
   waste production awareness use case, 34–35

Radius matching, 44
Random assignment, 19, 20f
Random forests, 71, 72–73, 75. *See also* Causal forests
   coupon campaign use case, 77, 82, 83–84
   pension plan participation use study, 95, 96–97
RDD. *See* Regression discontinuity designs
Regression analysis, 72
Regression discontinuity designs (RDD), 4–5
   behavioral assumptions and methods, 99, 102–107
   community development aid use case, 107–109, 109f
   fuzzy, 102, 104–105, 105f, 106
   local average treatment effect and, 103, 105
   loyalty card use cases, 100–101, 101f, 107
   overview of, 99–102, 101f
   pricing strategies, 101–102
   Python, use cases in, 109–110
   R software, use cases in, 107–109, 109f
   sharp, 99–101, 103–104, 104f, 106
Regression models
   in comparable groups in observed characteristics, 45–46
   errors, sensitivity to, 63–64
   inverse probability weighting, 48
   weighting and, 48
Restaurant e-coupons use case, 112
Ridge regression, 67–68
R software, use cases in, 2, 26–29
   in A/B testing, 29–33
   causal machine learning, 74–80
   community development aid use case, 107–109, 109f

coupon campaign use case, 50–54, 75–79
differences-in-differences, 117–119
double machine learning, 75–79, 76f
doubly robust estimation, 53
employment program use case, 118–119
instrumental variables, 93–95
inverse probability weighting, 52–53
lasso regression, 75
leaflet campaign use case, 29–31
local average treatment effect and, 93–95
newspaper advertising use case, 31–33, 32f, 33f
observational data, 49–54
pair matching, 51–52
pension plan participation use case, 93–95
policy trees, 79–80, 80f
regression discontinuity designs, 107–109, 109f
synthetic controls and, 128–130, 131f
tobacco control program use case, 128–130, 131f
Running variables, 99, 102, 103, 106. *See also* Index threshold; Time threshold

Sample, impact on, compared to population, 22–26
Sampling bias, 37
Selection bias, 12–17, 14f, 15f, 16f
Selection-on-observables assumption
   behavioral assumptions and, 41–42
   causal machine learning and, 60–61
   in differences-in-differences (DiD), 116–117
   failure of, 40–41, 41f
   pricing strategies and, 38–40, 39f
   synthetic controls, 126, 127
Selection-on-observables framework, 42–49, 43f
Sharp regression discontinuity designs, 99–101, 103–104, 104f, 106
Social media advertising, 40
Spillover effects, 10
Stable unit treatment value assumption (SUTVA), 10
Standard errors, 95, 130
Statistical independence ($\perp$), 22
Statistical significance, 31
Stepwise regression, 67
Stopping rules, 65
Streaming services, A/B testing and, 20
Subpopulations, 11, 61, 62f
SUTVA (stable unit treatment value assumption), 10
Synthetic controls method, 5–6, 125f
   behavioral assumptions and variants, 124–128
   differences-in-differences and, 123, 127, 131f, 132
   pricing strategies, 123–126
   Python, use cases in, 131–132
   R software, use cases in, 128–130, 131f
   selection-on-observables assumption, 126, 127
   single unit receives intervention, 123–124

Targeting strategy, optimization, 62–63, 73–74
Time index, 114
Time threshold, 101–102. *See also* Running variables

Tobacco control program use case
 Python, use cases in, 131–132
 R software, use cases in, 128–130, 131*f*
Train ticket discounts use case
 causal machine learning and, 61
 effect heterogeneity analysis and, 72–73
Treatment groups
 background characteristics, 12–15, 16*f*
 behavioral assumptions and, 41–42
 covariates and, 37–38, 38*f*
 in differences-in-differences approach, 111–113, 113*f*
 random assignment, 19, 20*f*
Two-stage regression approach, 91
Type I error probability, 25

Validation, 65, 67
Variables, notation for, 8–11, 9*f*
Variance, 25–26, 117

Waste production awareness use case, 34–35
Weak monotonicity assumption, 88
Wealth, as consumer characteristic, 59–60
Weighted averages, 124–126

Publisher contact:
The MIT Press
Massachusetts Institute of Technology
77 Massachusetts Avenue, Cambridge, MA 02139
mitpress.mit.edu

EU Authorised Representative:
Easy Access System Europe, Mustamäe tee 50,
10621 Tallinn, Estonia
gpsr.requests@easproject.com

Printed by Integrated Books International,
United States of America